Chronicles

of a

Skipper's Boy

1940 - 1945

Chronicles

of a

Skipper's Boy

1940 - 1945

Jan Deurwaarder

translated by

Betty Deurwaarder Forrester

English Translation Copyright 1998, 2010 by Jan Deurwaarder
First published in Dutch in 1996 by Schuttevaer Maritiem

Author's Dedication

To my two sisters and six brothers,
most of whom did not consciously experience
these recorded years
because they were still too young.

He who made the Pleiades and Orion,
who turns blackness into dawn
and darkens day into night,
who calls for the waters of the sea
and pours them out over the face of the land—
the Lord is His name.

Amos 5:8 (NIV)

Translator's Preface

It has been a privilege to translate my father's book. As much as possible I have stayed close to the original text, sometimes even literally translating an idiom in order to preserve the Dutch flavour. Some very common words such as 'Opoe,' Grandmother; 'Tante,' Aunt; and 'Oom,' Uncle, I have left untranslated.

Betty Deurwaarder Forrester
Vancouver, Canada
November, 1998

Table of Contents

Prologue: The Years Before the War of '40-'45 . . . . . *11*
    Jakob-Gerrit Deurwaarder
    Who was Neeltje Naeye?
    Together on the Orion

Care-free Youth	*18*
Heleentje	*22*
To School	*24*
In the Hospital	*27*
The Skippers' School	*30*
The First Year of the War	*32*
The Netherlands Capitulate	*37*
The Reunion	*37*
The Strange Barber	*40*
The Plane Disaster	*41*
The German Tugboat	*44*
Out of School at Last	*47*
A Cold Winter	*49*
The Shooting	*54*
Food Shortages in France	*60*
To Germany	*62*
The Ruhr	*70*
The Air Raid	*73*
Loading For IJmuiden	*79*
Firebombs.	*86*
Going Underground	*93*

Confiscated	96
Loading For Germany	98
On The Way To Magdenburg	101
The End Approaches	111
A Hard Night	115
The Move	117
Escape	120
Looking For A Place To Live	124
Life Of A Peaceful Countryman	130
Making Molasses	133
The Little White Church	135
The Betrayal	138
The Pipe Must Smoke	143
The Ammunition Train	145
The V1 And The V2	148
On A Bicycle Tour	150
The Ammunition Depot	151
The Liberation	159
Homeless Again	163
Father Looks For Work	168
The Foreman	171
Clean-up Of The War Damage	173
The Orion Is Found	175
The Fuss	179
A Hard Winter	182
Jan Leaves The Ship	188

Prologue

The Years Before the War of '40-'45

Jakob-Gerrit Deurwaarder

It was March 14, 1896. The Dutch towbarge Memento was moored in Duisburg-Ruhrort. On board that day Jakob-Gerrit first saw the light of day as the fifth child of the Deurwaarder family. Joy about this birth however was short-lived, because eight days later the mother passed away. In those days this was nothing short of a catastrophe.

For half a year his father and sisters took care of Jakob-Gerrit, but when the oldest daughter made it known that she wanted to leave the ship and did just that on arrival in Rotterdam, the problem became insurmountable. A hired hand was acquired to keep the Memento literally and figuratively afloat and father took care of the family—an impossible task. Initially housed with a foster mother, Jakob-Gerrit ended up with tante Helena after some detours.

Meanwhile father looked for a wife and mother for the family. He found her in the person we never knew other than 'Opoe Schot.' Typical of her was her pronouncement on her ninety-second birthday. When someone said to her, "You are old," she replied, "The devil is old."

Originally tante Helena lived in Overzande where her husband was a wagon maker. Shortly after they moved to Kloetinge, a village close to Goes and there Jakob-Gerrit went to school. Those were the happiest years of his youth, privileged as he was to live with tante Helena, who had no children of her own. His brothers Jan and Bram were soon through with studying because they had to work. And his sisters Nel and Neeltje had to learn on board ship, because that was too expensive on shore. Jakob-Gerrit on the other hand enjoyed adventures and roguish tricks. Such as noisily rattling sticks against the fence of the big church in the village square or secretly daring friends to see who could aim a good size jet over the top of the fully loaded cart of the green grocer.

But his fortune did not last long. Not yet nine years old, he had to come back to the Memento. Strangers off and family back on board. After all, family would work for room and board only. That is how the crisis around 1910 would be fought. It was hard work and long days for such a young boy. Hours on end at the helm in all kinds of weather manually turning the big steering wheel.

And when, at five o'clock in the morning, the tugboat sounded the first bell as a sign that they would sail at six o'clock, the anchor, heavy as lead, had to be pulled up by hand first. There was no difference between Sundays and workdays. A towbarge is after all dependent on the tugboat. That is where the decisions were made and waiting was not included. Even though Jakob-Gerrit did not know any better in those days, later this would be the occasion for far-reaching decisions.

He continued sailing until the start of the First World War. But, in spite of political neutrality, the Netherlands mobilized and he had to enter the army. Four whole years Jakob-Gerrit had to bear arms, of which the longest time was the guarding of the Belgian border. From 1918 until the beginning of 1927 he continued sailing on towbarges, mostly for his father, but also for strangers. He disliked the constant sailing on Sundays more and more.

He made plans to buy a self-propelled ship. After a few visits to the manager of the Dutch Ships Mortgage Bank in Rotterdam and after thorough deliberation with the manager of the shipyard Jansen in Druten, he got a mortgage. For 30,000 guilders a brand-new ship was built, 38 meters long and 5.05 meters wide, specially designed for sailing on the canals of France. Toward the end of 1927 it was ready for sailing.

The ship had to have a name of course. Probably Jakob-Gerrit thought about the many hours he sailed in the dark or stood watch under the clear starry skies, when he decided to name the ship after a constellation. Because the Bible also speaks of 'Orion' he chose this name.

During his conscription Jakob-Gerrit had regularly been to Bergen of Zoom. Faithfully he attended the church there, where the nurses from the psychiatric institution Vrederust also came regularly with their charges. He became fascinated with one of the nurses. She was called Neeltje Naeye and came from Axel, a small town in Zeeuws Vlaanderen. They met each other and an engagement soon followed. Because Jakob-Gerrit could not sail the Orion by himself they decided to get married. The wedding was solemnized on December 22, 1927 in Axel. A big change. Biggest for Neeltje, who traded her life as nurse for that of skipper's wife.

At the end of 1927 the Orion was ready to be launched

Who Was Neeltje Naeye?

Neeltje's father was a descendent of the Huguenots. His ancestors fled from France because of persecution and settled in Zaamslag, Zeeuws Vlaanderen. He taught himself the trade of cartwright. Neeltje's mother was born and raised in Axel. As the only child of a wealthy farmer's family, her childhood knew no worries. At a young age she married Jan Naeye, the wagon maker from Zaamslag. She brought along a sizable fortune. Jan Naeye knew what to do with that. He bought into a sawmill on the Kijkuit, a name that would rule Neeltje's life.

An economic recession soon announced itself and the sawmill went bankrupt. Jan Naeye picked up his old trade as wagon maker again. The family continued to live in Kijkuit and expanded to seven children. Every weekday Neeltje walked with her brothers and sisters to school in Axel—one hour there in the morning and one back in the afternoon. In the winter always in the dark and in wooden shoes. On Sunday they walked the same distance to church, but then they got home earlier. They suffered dire poverty. Thanks to their own garden, baking their own bread, and gifts from farmers, they survived those years.

When Neeltje's elementary schooldays were over, her father traded the business on the Kijkuit for a cartwright shop in Axel. But here too, almost supernatural efforts were necessary to survive. One of the heaviest tasks of Neeltje and her mother was helping to saw logs. With a tackle the log had to be pulled onto the staging, about one and a half meters high. Father stood on the staging and both women on the ground, between them an enormous saw blade, which, by pulling back and forth, would cut a log in pieces lengthwise. As Neeltje grew up, the question came up of what she would do. Staying at home was not possible. Food and clothing could not be provided for everyone in the family.

Here was a dilemma. Some older sisters had left home already. Neeltje's oldest sister, Bep, was a nurse in Vrederust in Bergen of Zoom. She asked the matron if Neeltje could come and work there as well. And, yes, that was allowed. The transition from the sheltered home life to a psychiatric institution, then still called lunatic asylum, must have been very big for Neeltje. In spite of all the difficulties some funny incidents occurred. For example there was the time during the church service…

For several weeks Neeltje had taught two patients from different groups a line of a children's rhyme. During the church service, just before the start of the sermon, she said to the girl sitting next to her, "Call out what I taught you."

"I don't dare to," the girl answered.

"Then I'll pinch your arm," Neeltje threatened.

The girl, apparently scared of that, called out, "Sweetie pie, are you still alive?"

From the other side of the church, where the second girl was sitting the answer came, "Yes sir, I'm still here!" Much hilarity, except for the minister.

And then Neeltje met the love of her life.

Together On The Orion

The first years on the Orion were very difficult—low freight prices and much down-time because of engine problems. A large German factory, Gorlitz, had delivered and installed the 80 hp engine. And even though the factory had installed heavy engines of 5000 hp for foreign power plants, they could not get this midget of 80 hp to work properly. Several engineers of the factory were on board the ship day and night to hunt for and repair the defects. Sailing in the daytime and fixing by night. There was no end to the misery and finally it could not go on this way.

In 1930 Jakob-Gerrit went to the bank with lead in his shoes. After explaining everything he asked the bank to give him a second mortgage. His request was accepted and he chose a radical solution. The German engine was removed and an engine of Dutch make, from Appingedam, went in its place. That was how the misery ended.

In spite of all the reverses and problems nature took its course. In November 1928 the first child was born, Gezina Maria Elisabeth, in daily life 'Ina.' Nine more would follow.

Care-free Youth

A sing-song voice woke Jan that beautiful summer morning, "Wake up, the sun is shining, the birds are singing in the tree-tops."

At the same time he heard the soft droning of a diesel engine and he knew he was back on board a ship. He threw off the blankets, opened the curtains in front of the port-hole and saw the shore gliding by.

He quickly dressed himself and ran to the cockpit, where father stood at the helm. He steered the Orion through the French canal of Saint Quentin, on the way to Paris. One week earlier the Orion had loaded 150 rolls of newsprint in Velsen, near Ijmuiden. The hold was totally filled and rolls stuck up above the spar. There they were covered with tarps so they would not get wet.

Shortly after Jan, mother entered the cockpit with tea and bread.

"I thought you were still in bed," mother said to Jan.

"No way," Jan answered, "I heard you singing and quickly jumped out of bed. The others are still sleeping."

"Here is tea and bread, enjoy it," mother said, passing him a plate and a cup. Father shifted the engine to 'slow.' Jan looked through the front window of the cockpit and saw a lock a short distance in front of the ship. The lock-gates were still closed and so they would have to be patient. In the meantime more children had woken up; his sister Ina and younger brother Wim. Jan, who by now had emptied his plate, asked father if he could go on shore to help the lock-keeper open the lock-gates.

"Very well," father said, "you help that man, otherwise he has to walk all the way around to open the other door and that only takes longer."

The deck-hand helped Jan on shore with the boom and Jan ran to the lock. He waved to the lock-keeper on the other side of the lock who waved back and made a turning motion toward the crank with which the lock-gates are opened and closed. Little Jan stretched, took hold of the crank and started to turn. Slowly the lock-gate started to move and opened more all the time.

While turning Jan looked at the lock-keeper out of the corner of his eye. He looked poor and very shabbily dressed. All of a sudden Jan saw that the man had only one leg. The second one was not there. From the knee down there was no leg or foot to be seen, only a wooden stick. It looked like a broomstick. Perplexed Jan forgot to turn the crank. The lock-keeper saw Jan looking confused, started to laugh and said something in French. Jan could not understand any of it. He took hold of the crank again and turned the lock-gates open without stopping.

When both gates were open, the Orion carefully sailed into the lock. Jan admired his father, because there was very little room to steer the ship into the lock. After the ship was tied up Jan again helped the lock-keeper to close the lock-gates.

When the Orion had sailed out of the lock a little later and Jan had gone back to his spot in the cockpit, he asked his mother, "Why does that man have such a strange leg?"

Mother had to laugh and said, "On many locks in France people work who were soldiers in the First World War. They were wounded and some lost an arm or a leg and, yes, there were also some who lost an eye. After the war many of these people were given work on the locks and bridges, so they could take care of their families themselves. But they earn so little that they can't buy decent clothes. That's why these people get a few francs from most of the skippers who pass by, you understand?"

No, Jan did not understand at all, he was only five years old.

After sailing for weeks and passing countless locks, in the course of which they had to lay still for a long time because of a strike by angry French skippers, the Orion reached Paris.

It was Friday afternoon when father reported to the office to unload.

"You'll have to wait with unloading till Monday morning; the workers have gone home," the boss there said. "Moor your ship on the other side of the canal near that demolition yard. It is quieter there than here."

When father got back on board the engine was started and the Orion sailed to the other side of the canal. The ship was tied up at the car demolition yard.

"Come on, Jan," father said, "quickly wash and change then we'll go on shore to get bread, Wim can come too."

In the meantime six o'clock came and the people of the demolition yard went home. When father and Jan came back on deck to go on shore they heard terrible growling on shore. There two large guard dogs with flashing teeth were waiting for them.

"Papa, shouldn't Wim and I stay on board to look after mama?" Jan said.

"You do that and I'll stay on board to look after you, how about that?" father answered.

Not till Monday morning when the workmen came back, were the dogs locked up in their kennel. The children did not mind it very much. Mother had made pancakes and that was a treat. When the paper was unloaded, after a week of waiting, coke was loaded for Strassbourg. Again they passed a large number of locks and the children enjoyed it when they were allowed to walk along from one lock to another and could gather apples on the way.

After the coke was unloaded the empty ship sailed on the Rhine to Mannheim. The Rhine was so low however that a pilot came along to show the way. Sometimes they felt the ship scraping over the sand. In Mannheim the ship was loaded for Rotterdam. And after a round-trip of about three months the Orion arrived there again.

In February 1933 the Orion moored in Terneuzen.

"Listen," mother said to the children, "I'm going to stay with Oma in Axel for a week. Only Ina can come, the boys will stay with father. And when I come back I'll have a surprise. Then I'll bring back a new little brother or sister. Deal?"

Jan and Wim blushed and gave each other a shove. But Ina was already packing her bag. They all took mother and Ina to the steam tram and waved good-bye. Ten days later father picked mother and Ina up again and what did they bring? A little brother and his name was Johan.

Father had gotten impatient waiting for ten days. Quickly a grocery list was made that was taken to Bareman the grocer by the deck-hand. "And please deliver it by tonight."

"No problem," the grocer answered.

Early the next morning the engine was started and they left Terneuzen in the direction of Paris.

Heleentje

The depression years were severe and difficult. There was a four to six week wait for a load. And the charterers who offered the skippers work were usually to be found in the pub. The skipper who was generous with his offer of alcohol or beer money was the first to get the work. But the good charterers didn't operate this way. When after weeks of waiting you got a load you sailed long days to get rid of it as soon as possible, after which more weeks of waiting and idleness followed.

Meanwhile the year 1935 came. Sister Rie, born in 1934, celebrated her first birthday. Once in a while Jan heard his parents talking with each other about the way Germany was busy reinforcing her armies. The Germans were also involved in enlarging their borders. A part of Poland had already been added to Germany that way. Those who defended themselves were shot or interred in a labor camp. Europe trembled with fear. But Jan heard his father say, "They won't do anything to our country, we'll stay neutral, just like in 1914-1918." And despite all the somber newscasts the Orion continued making her trips to France.

In 1937 after loading on the river De Schelde in Belgium, the Orion sailed towards Paris. Heleentje, born in 1936, was having her afternoon nap in her crib, which stood on a fixed bench, while mother was busy with her work. There was always much to do that could only be done when the littlest one was out of the way. The front of the crib, a gate, was fastened with two hooks. When you took off the gate the crib was lower and it was easier to get at the baby.

Suddenly mother heard a bang behind her. When she looked up she saw that the gate was gone and that Heleentje was laying on the floor. She got a scare and when she picked the child up it lay limp in her arms. Carefully she put Heleentje down and sent Ina upstairs to call father.

"Take the helm," father said to the deck-hand and went to the deck-house.

"It doesn't look good," he said to mother, "we should quickly get a doctor."

Father went upstairs and stopped the ship. With a steel cable around a tree the ship was tied up. He sent the deck-hand on shore to get the doctor. Fortunately they were not far from a village called Sichem. The doctor was found quickly and came right away with the deck-hand. He examined Heleentje, but could not give any hope.

"She fell on her head and is in a deep coma. We can't move her. Leave her lying down and wait and see," he advised.

After father and mother watched all night Heleentje died early in the morning. Opa came over from Axel and attended the funeral. She was buried in Sichem on the extreme edge of the cemetery.

"Protestants may not be buried in the hallowed ground of the cemetery," the priest said.

To School

In November Ina turned seven and according to mother it was time that she went to school. Because she pitied her going by herself, she suggested to father that Jan be sent along. Father did not like the idea at all and objected.

"We earn little and two children in school costs a lot."

But mother insisted. "We already have so little room with five children. We have to make do more and more here on board."

She wrote a letter to her parents in Axel and asked if Ina and Jan could come and stay at their house in order to go to school. Opa wrote back that that was fine and that they could come for the new school year. He was glad that this way they would have some extra income. As wagon maker it was difficult to earn a living and when you yourself have two big boys in college every bit of income is welcome.

Ina and Jan went to school. They got new clothes and shoes for church and wooden shoes to go to school. In first grade Miss Flipse was boss. She took Jan under her wing. She had an understanding for the problems of a six year old away from home for the first time, and protected him from pushy children. For the rest of his life he remembered her as the most loving school teacher. Ina soon had a friend, called Zus van Driel, a shoemaker's daughter who lived two houses away from Opa.

Whenever the Orion was in the neighborhood, bags full of groceries were dropped off for Oma. Including, for example, sandwich spreads, because Oma had nothing else to spread on the bread than lard. Only on Sunday was there sometimes a piece of bacon to go with it or a slice of bread was topped with brown sugar.

Jan and Ina always watched with excitement to see how Oma buttered and cut the big round loaves. The round bread, baked by herself on a stone, was held against her chest. With the bread knife the lard was spread on while the crumbs flew in every direction and then a slice was cut off. It is no wonder her left thumb sometimes got too close to the knife and it goes without saying that the piece of bread would sometimes get red.

On Saturday when there was no school, Jan was always in high spirits. All day he could be found close to Opa. Opa worked just as hard on Saturday as on any other day. Sometimes he had to help. Then Opa put a log on two wooden trestles, climbed on top and took an enormous cross-cut saw. Oma and Jan stood on the floor and took the other handle of the cross-cut saw in their hands. And then the heavy work started. Jan's mother had done this too in the past. The log was sawn in two lengthwise. They were exhausted afterwards. Then Opa took a plane of one meter length to make the board smooth. Sometimes Jan was allowed to help bring a handcart of stove wood to the church. Then he helped Opa push the loaded cart over the bumpy stones and on the way home he was allowed to sit in the cart. The most dangerous moment came when the heavy laden cart had to go down the steep sloping walkway to the basement of the church. As soon as the cart started to go down Opa and Jan had to hang onto the handles so that the legs of the cart dragged over the stones and the cart was slowed down.

On Sunday afternoons Opa, Ina and Jan often went for a short walk. Along the creek, by a large pond, was a walking path with a high hedge next to it. One time a man on a bike came up behind them and passed weaving by them. Opa shook his head.

"How can people do such a thing and that on Sunday."

Soon after the man suddenly veered to the right and drove into the hedge. Jan thought it a comical sight and roared with laughter. Opa looked up and saw what had happened. He pulled Jan to him and boxed his ears.

"How dare you laugh at something like that," he said, "and that on Sunday. Come on, we're going home."

When they got home again, Oma asked why they were back so soon. In the kitchen Ina quietly told her what had happened. By the look on Oma's face Ina could tell that she did not think it was as bad as Opa did.

In the Hospital

One Sunday something awful happened. After the meal, baked beans with a piece of bacon, Jan got a terrible stomach pain. It quickly got worse and Opa decided to get the doctor. The doctor arrived quickly and diagnosed appendicitis. It was, however, so acute that the doctor feared a rupture. There was no time to call a taxi and after Oma quickly gathered some nightclothes, Jan was laid on the back seat of the doctor's beautiful car. Opa took his seat next to the doctor and with great speed they went to the hospital in Sluiskil.

When Jan looked up again he did not know what he saw. Two women with black wimples on their heads bent over him and lifted him out of the car. He was put on a cart and quickly they rode him into the hospital. He did not know what was going on and in order not to cry he closed his eyes. Before they wheeled him into the operating room he felt someone touch his arm. Jan looked up and saw that it was Opa.

"Oh, good," Jan thought, "Opa is still here."

"So long, boy," Opa said, "be brave."

The operation was done quickly and was successful according to the doctor. But the incision had to be kept partly open for a week for drainage. Fortunately for Jan the Orion was in Terneuzen that week and father and mother were able to come for a visit.

"Well, Jan," father said, "you deserve a nice present, what would you like?"

"A train on a track," Jan said.

"Fine," father said, "I'll have a look if that is available."

The next day father, mother, Ina and Wim came for a visit and father put a big box on the bed. Jan wanted to sit up right away, but oh, how his belly hurt. While lying down he opened the box and could not believe his eyes. In the box he saw a beautiful train. A locomotive, a coal wagon and two carriages. They were a beautiful color and gleamed in the light. Father laid down the track on the floor and let the train make a few rounds. Jan's eyes shone. After two weeks of good care from the nuns Jan was allowed to go home again.

Later Wim, the younger brother of Ina and Jan, also came to live with Opa and Oma in Axel to go to school. Oom Wim, the second youngest son of Opa, thought it wonderful to have a namesake at home. In Opa's house there was a big tiled hall with a staircase with fifteen steps to the second floor. Several times Oom Wim put little Wim on his shoulders and carried him up and down the stairs that way. Little Wim had a lot of fun.

Until something went wrong. Oom Wim came down the stairs with little Wim on his shoulders. He had only taken a few steps when he tripped and fell down the stairs, hit his head on the tiled floor, and lay motionless. It was a miracle that little Wim escaped with a scare, but Oom Wim had a concussion and had to lie flat for two weeks.

The attic at Opa and Oma's was spooky. The first year Jan and Ina slept in the same room. There was no electric light. With a kerosene lamp the children were brought to bed, after which the light was placed in the hall downstairs. When they were in bed there was always something to hear. Birds under the roof tiles or mice in the garret. Sometimes they got a scare because the bedroom door softly opened and Oom Fien, mother's youngest brother, would throw an apple, that he had taken from the garret, onto the bed.

One evening, Ina lay alone in her room and Jan and Wim in the bedroom next to it, when the whole house started to shake and tremble and the windows rattled. Quickly they jumped out of bed to see if maybe a big truck was passing by. But there was nothing to see. While they stood in front of the window, Oma hastily came into the room and said, "Quickly get your clothes, there is an earthquake, come downstairs right away."

In the hall they waited for a while, but nothing else happened. Opa finally took them back to bed.

The Skippers' School

Meanwhile father and mother had made plans to place Ina and Jan in a school where they would not have to stay for six years, but where they would learn just as much in three years. It would not be possible to keep all the children in school for six years. The school they were looking for had to be located on a route regularly traveled by the Orion. The choice went to Wemeldinge. The principal of the school had a sister who was widowed at a young age and he asked her to act as foster mother. And so it happened that Jan, who was now eight years old, and Ina, went to a different school.

The new foster mother and the different school brought a big change into their lives. From now on they went to school three times a day and also on Saturday morning. They had to work hard and did not have much time for play. At the same time you always had to be on guard for the children of the other school. They looked on the skippers' children as interlopers in their village life and thought they had to resist them by fighting. Especially in the winter months when darkness came early and Jan and Ina went home in the dark, they had to be extra careful.

Once they walked home together from school and could be heard from far away by the stomping of their wooden shoes. Suddenly, around the corner of a store boys from the other school jumped out and wanted to bother Ina. Even though Jan was no hero and could run fast he did not want to desert his sister. Fortunately he had a few days earlier found a piece of broken strap from a bicycle and put it in his pocket. Before the boys realized what was happening they one by one got a smack with the rubber. That stopped them in their tracks and to the big relief of the duo they quickly took to their heels.

The First Year of the War

The spring of 1940 was, in spite of the beautiful weather, a tense time. There was whispering and gossiping, and rumors were spread. Nobody trusted anybody. Everyone saw in his neighbor a German spy and kept him at a distance. One had to be on guard.

Faithfully Jan went to school three times a day together with his sister. A fifteen minute walk there and a fifteen minute walk back. Fortunately winter was past and they did not have to go home in the dark anymore. April passed and May made her entrance. Nature was wearing her most beautiful robe. The fruit trees were in full bloom and you could smell the hawthorn from afar.

But the rumors that Germany wanted to start a war increased. A partial unleashing of the aggression had already taken place at the eastern borders of Germany. Enlarging territory was number one. Opposition was put down with a heavy hand.

On May 10th, early in the morning, the man next door entered Jan and Ina's foster home and called, "Neighbors, the Germans have attacked the Netherlands. At Venlo they have crossed the border in an armored train. On the Grebbe mountain there is heavy fighting and parachutists have been dropped at the Moerdijk bridges."

Their foster mother was seized with alarm.

"What now? Strange children in the home and no knowing where the parents are."

On top of that a large lock complex lay at a distance of a twenty minute walk, which the Germans would want to put out of action as soon as possible.

Tante De Vos, as the foster mother was called, decided to leave the house together with Jan and Ina and move farther away from the locks. And that is what happened. Ina and Jan each got a little suitcase with clothes to carry, tante De Vos took the large suitcase herself and that is how they set out.

In the meantime there was total chaos. No Germans had yet been seen when the French soldiers came to help the Netherlands and started to shoot at random. French airplanes flew back and forth over the locks and the canal. Many ships looked for a safe haven or tried to reach their home-port. The waterways swarmed with Belgian and French ships wanting to go South.

After about an hour's walk the trio arrived at a farm far away from the village. The farmer was busy behind the barn, covering a large pit of about one meter depth with old doors and planks. On top of that he threw a layer of dirt and that way a primitive bomb shelter was created. Tante De Vos asked the farmer, who she knew well, if she and the children could stay with him because the village so close to the locks was too dangerous.

"Oh, well," the farmer said, "I made this shelter really for my family, but I understand that you need a place too. I say crawl in, and if necessary we can fit in as well. After all, many tame sheep fit in a pen. If you wait a minute I'll get some straw. We'll put that on the floor first against the cold."

Of course Tante De Vos thanked the farmer profusely for his hospitality. Straw was close at hand for the farmer, so a thick layer was quickly put down. Through a small entrance they crawled inside one by one. Ina and Jan thought it very exciting. It seemed a little like they were camping.

They could not stand up straight, space did not permit that. The suitcases were dragged inside and put against the side. While they were still busy the farmer's wife came to have a look. She had heard from her husband what was happening.

"Do you want to sleep here as well?" she asked Tante De Vos.

"We'll have to," she replied. I don't dare go home for the time being. If the Germans bomb the locks we would be much too close."

"But then I'll first get some blankets for you," the farmer's wife said, "you can't just lie on the straw, you would get sick."

Soon after, the farmer's wife came back with a pile of blankets, a loaf of bread, a bottle of milk, and a white chamber pot.

"There you go," the farmer's wife said, "this will do you for the time being. If you need something just send one of the children."

Tante De Vos thanked the farmer's wife heartily. Everything went into the shelter except for the white chamber pot. It was put next to the entrance of the bomb shelter, so that in case of need it would be ready. By noon everything was prepared and while waiting for the coming events they had a sandwich. What a long day.

At a distance of about three hundred meters from the bomb shelter was a road leading to the lock complex in the village. On this road a long column of military vehicles and soldiers went in the direction of the locks. The French had to stop the Germans and if possible turn them back. French airplanes also flew over regularly. They could track down and intercept possible German troop movement. Jan watched with his hands above his eyes.

Suddenly one of the airplanes dove down and came at high speed in the direction of the bomb shelter where the three of them were watching.

"Inside," Tante De Vos screamed, "they're going to shoot!"

Head first Ina and Jan dove into the bomb shelter, followed by Tante De Vos who was hampered by her big cap and wide skirt. At the same time machine-gun fire crackled from the plane and the soil flew around. Fortunately the bomb shelter was not hit, but it was a close call.

After the airplane passed and the shooting stopped Tante De Vos went outside to see if it was safe. To her alarm she saw that the plane turned in a wide circle and intended to start another dive.

"Why are they shooting at our bomb shelter?" she thought.

Fearfully she looked around and then saw next to the entrance the white chamber pot flickering in the fierce sunlight.

"That's it!" she thought, "they think of course that it is a signal for the Germans." She grabbed a wooden crate that lay next to the pot and threw it on top so it could not be seen anymore.

And indeed, when she looked up she saw the plane end its dive and fly away to the west. A sigh of relief escaped her. The farmer came in a hurry to look around the corner of the barn and called, "What happened? It looks like they were plowing, the whole field is upside down."

"Oh," Tante De Vos said, "but they didn't quite finish."

That afternoon was a holiday for Ina and Jan. Beautiful weather and walking around freely on a farm, isn't that great? Jan went along with the farmer to get feed for the cows with the horse and wagon. And Ina went with the farmer's wife to feed the chickens and geese and gather the eggs. She was allowed to take an egg for each of them. But Tante De Vos did not know how to boil or fry them for there was no fire.

These were nerve-wracking days for Tante De Vos. What would she do with someone else's children if war broke out? Would the parents still return? Or would they maybe be forced to sail for Germany? Questions, questions without an answer. She could not do anything but wait and see and hope for better times.

Life was one big adventure now for the children, so they hardly had time to think of the Orion. It was moored in the Axelse Sassing, a little dead-end harbor about five kilometers outside the village of Axel. That is where they had been sent to from Sluiskil where they first had moored. At six o'clock in the morning Opa already stood by the ship to tell them that the war with Germany had started.

Because ships are an easy target for airplanes, it was decided to temporarily go on shore. Shelter was found with a farmer in a barn and the first days of the war were awaited there until after capitulation.

The Netherlands Capitulate

That is how May 15, 1940 arrived. The three in the bomb shelter woke up early. The sun was shining and the lovely scent of the hawthorn in full bloom enticed them outside from their stuffy space.

Stretching themselves and still stiff from the unusual posture on the straw they crawled on their knees through the small exit. Jan made sure he was the first one outside but when he wanted to stand up he saw a pair of wooden shoes right in front of his nose. When he looked up he saw two legs and got a scare. Then he saw it was the farmer.

Jan smiled at him, but did not dare to say anything, the farmer looked so strange. After the others had also crawled out of the bomb shelter the farmer said to Tante De Vos, "I have bad news for you. Yesterday afternoon the Germans bombed Rotterdam. There are many dead and wounded. The whole inner-city is on fire. The Dutch government capitulated this morning and the Queen left for England."

Tante De Vos blanched with fear. "Does, does that mean that the Netherlands will be occupied by the Germans?"

"Yes, unfortunately," the farmer said, "but take it easy and be careful. And if you ever need anything feel free to drop by, because times may yet be very difficult." After Tante De Vos had provided breakfast to the best of her abilities, they got ready to leave. They said good-bye to the farmer and his wife. Tante De Vos thanked them for their hospitality and promised to come back sometime. After that they headed back.

Soon after Tante De Vos arrived back home with Ina and Jan the Netherlands was overrun by German soldiers. All French and Dutch soldiers were made prisoners of war and had to turn in their weapons. In long lines they stumbled along the road to be interned. Large hangars and halls were equipped to house them. Despite the quick conquest many were killed. They were buried together at the back of the cemetery. Much later, for those who were not transported home, an honorary cemetery would be constructed.

The Reunion

After a week Tante De Vos' doorbell rang. And who were standing on the steps? Father and mother! How happy Jan and Ina were to be able to see everyone in good health again. Father told them they had hoped to be able to be in Holland before the Germans arrived. But when they got to Sluiskil on the way back from France, the Dutch authorities would not allow them to continue and they were sent to the Axelse Sassing. Because of the quick advance and occupation by the Germans they had only had to wait two days. And then they were allowed to sail on to Terneuzen.

Because the locks in Terneuzen and Hansweert were almost totally intact, they could sail on to Wemeldinge the next day and that is why they had arrived already. Fortunately they had not encountered anything serious and they were in good health.

"Then we can come along now to the Orion?" Jan asked.

"That's allowed," father said, "until Monday. Then we continue and then you go back to school."

"Hooray," Jan shouted, "Are you coming, Ina?"

But before they knew it the weekend was over and they had to go back to Tante De Vos.

The Strange Barber

Ina and Jan noticed little of the German occupation. They heard talk about N.S.B.-ers* and turncoats and girls going steady with Germans, but the gist of it passed them by. They were still too young. When everything was back to normal Tante De Vos said to Jan one day, "Tomorrow is Wednesday and then you get home from school at three o'clock. Come home at once to get money, then you can go to the barber. It's about time."

So the next day Jan went to the barber, the only one in the village. Jan noticed that the barber acted differently than before. While he cut Jan's hair he said that his part was not right. It should be on the right side, where Hitler's part was too. Without further talk he suited his words to the deed and put the part on the right side. When Jan got home Tante De Vos noticed right away that Jan's hair was different than before.

"Why is that?" she asked.

"The barber says everybody should wear their part on the right side, because that's what Hitler does," Jan answered.

"Yes, yes," she said, "I knew he was a N.S.B.-er, but I didn't expect him to put it into practice."

---

* Members of the Netherlands Socialist Party, looked on as traitors, because they collaborated with the Germans.

The Plane Disaster

The first years of the war passed by quietly for Ina, Jan and Wim (who in the meantime also went to school in Wemeldinge). School and holiday times alternated. They regularly went with the Orion, but that always passed too quickly for their liking. Once, during the summer vacation—which in those days lasted till the end of August—something terrible happened in the always quiet village.

In the middle of the night everyone woke with a scare from the sound of a very low-flying plane. It flew so low that it must hit the tops of the trees. Suddenly there was an enormous bang, after which there were a few seconds of dead-silence. Immediately after the sky turned red with the flames and they even shone through the skylight of the attic where the children were sleeping. They jumped out of bed and quickly grabbed their clothes and threw them over their arms as they ran down the steep stairs. Tante De Vos had already gotten out of bed as well and stood looking out of the window.

"Can I go outside?" asked Jan, after getting dressed.

"Yes," Tante De Vos said, "but not by yourself, we'll come too. Everybody quickly put on your coat because it's cold out on the street at night."

The four of them walked to the Wilhelmina street, where the fire was raging. At a good distance from the crashed plane they were stopped and were not allowed to go on. They could feel the heat in their faces. It was an English airplane that had crashed into four of a row of houses. The fire brigade was present, but could do very little. The sea of fire was tremendous. They were also afraid of exploding ammunition that was still in the plane and flying around.

The firemen tried to save the inhabitants of the collapsed houses, but had to pull back because of the enormous heat. When the fire burned out after many hours, the charred bodies of the airplane crew were recovered by the German soldiers. They would not say how many people were involved. In the destroyed houses the remains of four occupants were found. After a few weeks, when everything was cleaned up, the village showed a serious war scar.

Only after the war did it become known that the plane was a Vickers Wellington MK.Ic., a plane that should have a six man crew. However only five were found. They were buried in Vlissingen. The plane was returning from a bombing expedition over Dusseldorf.

In the middle of the night everyone woke with a scare to the noise of a very low-flying airplane.

The German Tugboat

One dreary day Jan was sauntering on the locks to see which ships were moored or passing. In the back of his head he always had a quiet hope that the Orion would be there. You never knew where they might suddenly come from. On one trip artificial fertilizer was taken to France and they returned with wheat for Groningen. On another trip they brought sand or gravel from the west coast of Belgium and came back with cement from Obourg for Zwolle. Any moment they could arrive on the doorstep. The least fun however was when the Orion arrived on Wednesday afternoon and had to leave early the next morning to have a favorable tide. Ina, Jan and Wim could not sleep on board then and had to go back to their boarding house in order to go to bed on time.

But this time everything went differently. Dejectedly Jan walked over the lock-gates to go back home. Suddenly at a little distance he heard a lot of commotion. People were pointing to the mouth of the harbor and stood busily gesturing. Jan also looked in that direction and saw a Dutch tugboat that had been claimed by the Germans sailing into the harbor. It was painted totally grey.

But Jan also saw that the people who had been talking a little earlier were roughly chased away by a number of German soldiers. Jan did not lose a moment and quickly went to stand behind the hut of the lock-workers. He was lucky. The Germans did not see him.

The tugboat in the meantime slowly sailed closer by. The soldiers got more and more nervous and ran back and forth like fools. On both sides of the tugboat Jan saw dark objects floating that were tied to the rail with a rope. Jan got more curious all the time and stuck out his head as far as possible in order not to miss anything. Fortunately the soldiers did not see him. The tugboat got so close that Jan could clearly recognize the floating objects beside the tugboat. He almost had to vomit with fright when he saw what they were.

Human heads! Seven of them. Horrible. Pilots in their partly air-filled uniforms bobbed like floats next to the tugboat. One by one they were hauled out of the water, laid on a stretcher and pushed into waiting trucks. A little later the trucks drove quickly away accompanied by a motor-escort. Feeling sick from what he had seen Jan ran as fast as he could. He had to make a big detour in order not to have to pass the soldiers.

The next day rumors spread in the village that the night before an English plane had to make an emergency landing on a dry sand bank. The Germans were posted on this and laid a cordon of armed patrol boats around the sand bank and the airplane. They shot at anything that moved. Escape was impossible. After some time the tide came in and the airplane filled up. The crew had nowhere to go and drowned. The underground, knowing about the airplane, tried to reach the pilots from St. Philipsland to rescue them, but they too did not have a chance.

Without pausing to consider Jan quickly went and stood behind the hut of the lock workers

- 46 -

Out of School at Last

In the summer of 1943 Jan was finally allowed out of school. His sister Ina had gone back to the ship the year before. In the meantime Johan and Rie were ready for school and moved into the house of Tante De Vos. Jan was twelve years old and plenty big and strong he thought, to become his father's deckhand on the Orion.

The first trip they went with sand to the little town of Betune in Northern France. After the Orion was unloaded and had a big clean-up there was still one thing to do before Sunday. The water tank had to be filled. The Orion was moored as close as possible near the water pump and the water was carried on board ship with buckets. A heavy chore.

To fill the buckets with water a big knob on top of the pump had to be pushed in. Because Jan was not tall he could hardly reach the knob. He put a bucket under the pump and decided to climb on top and then stand on it with his foot. The pump would then continue to give water. Jan could not carry any buckets himself then, but he thought his father would think it easier not to have to push the knob every time. And it worked.

Triumphantly Jan stood on top of the pump and the water streamed uninterruptedly. But always standing on one leg is very difficult when you are not a stork. After several buckets were filled Jan wanted to stand on his other leg for a change. He moved his left foot in order to put his right foot in its place and then it happened. His shoes had become very slippery because of the water and slid away.

He tumbled down and broke his wrist. No lack of crying. Father quickly got his bike from the ship. Jan was put on the back and so they went to the hospital. After the wrist had been set in a cast they went back on board ship. Jan would not be able to do much for his father.

Several hours later however it appeared that the fingers sticking out of the cast were swelling up because the cast was too tight. After two days it was decided to look for a doctor. The Orion was moored and father and Jan went to a doctor. The doctor was afraid for the now blue fingers. He took a pair of scissors and cut the cast open lengthwise. That was a relief. But it took six more weeks before the cast could come off all the way.

During these six weeks Jan had promised his mother to work for her for the rest of his life when he was better. He would peel potatoes, wash windows, get the groceries and much more. But as soon as the cast came off those good intentions were forgotten.

A Cold Winter

Winter came closer quickly. The population of all of Europe was dreading it. What would happen? There was little fuel, food kept getting scarcer, and clothing was hardly to be had.

And how much longer would it last? One heard rumors about the German front in Russia and Africa. When you listened to German radio Hitler's army was winning on all fronts, but the few individuals who could receive the BBC (the English radio) knew better than that. Then there was the fear of the Germans of an invasion by the Allied troops on the coasts of France and Belgium. And in their terror the Germans raged like beasts.

The Jews especially had a rough time. Millions of men, women and even children were taken and transported just because they were Jews. Who could ever have foreseen the price they had to pay for their lineage? But also resistance fighters were taken to concentration camps in large numbers. People suspected something terrible was going on, but how terrible only came to light after the war. Then it became clear how much havoc the Nazis caused.

The Orion made several trips together with the Corati on which friends of father and mother sailed. They took sand, gravel or cement in bags to the Belgian coast and northern

France. With might and main the Germans strengthened the Atlantic Wall. Rumors were going around that there were some skippers who tried to sabotage the operation by mixing into the loads small amounts of sugar. Small amounts were enough to stop the cement and sand from drying. This made the concrete brittle and it did not get hard. The amounts of sand and cement supplied were however so large that insufficient sugar, which was rationed after all, could be hauled in.

Father and mother discussed with their friends the question of whether or not one could sail for the Germans. If you were forced could you then accept money? And if you sailed voluntarily for them did you not aid the oppressor?

But however consistent you were you could not keep up the resistance for very long. Both had large families and many mouths to feed. But sometimes they had a stroke of luck. During a trip of the Orion on the Maas, as it turned to dusk, father said: "If I'm not mistaken my brother Bram is sailing in front of us on the Vios." And sure enough, when they came closer they recognized each other. Both ships stopped and lowered their anchors to spend the night next to each other.

Hearty greetings followed. They had not seen each other for a long time and now such an unexpected meeting. When the brothers had been talking together for a little while father called Jan.

"Come lad," he said, "before we eat we have a little job to do."

Jan wondered what that could be. His uncle opened the coal storage on board of his ship and said, "You may take half of the coal. After the last trip some coal was left in the hold that we saved, leftovers from the load. To throw it overboard at such a time as this would be a pity, so there you go."

That did not fall on deaf ears. Jan filled the buckets and his father carried them on board the Orion. They were hidden well in the engine room, otherwise there was a chance that they would be stolen. How happy mother was. The supply had dwindled quite a bit after all. They had an evening of pleasant conversation. The ships separated the next morning and everyone continued his trip.

After the Orion had been unloaded in Rotterdam artificial fertilizer was loaded in the Wilhelmina harbor in Vlaardingen for Kampen. Father said that for the whole trip only 1200 liters of fuel were available and that was not enough to sail to Kampen. He was planning to sail to Rotterdam under his own power and then have a tugboat take us upstream to Arnhem. From the IJsselkop at Arnhem we could sail on downstream by ourselves. And that is how it happened. In Rotterdam a tow was assembled out of three ships that all together carried about one thousand tons.

The next day, there was a hard frost. Sailing started early. At eight o'clock they sailed up the river Lek. The weather turned beautifully clear with bright sunshine. The tugboat had trouble pulling three ships against the current. The further they went the more difficult it became. There was one advantage. In Wageningen one of the ships would stay behind to unload.

Father nervously walked back and forth behind the helm while his pipe smoked just as much as the chimney of the tugboat. What could be the matter, Jan wondered? Then he heard father say to mother, "I hope no English fighters will come and shoot at us, because we're like sitting ducks and can't go anywhere. I would make the shelter ready in the deck-house, you never know." Mother went into the deck-house and put the table in a corner next to the couch. Mattresses and beds were laid on top of the table. In case of an emergency mother and the children could crawl under the table. They were safer there than on deck or in the cockpit.

After sailing for a day and a half, the tugboat with the two ships arrived safely at the IJsselkop. The Orion was thrown loose from the tug and sailed under its own power further down the IJssel. With the current they sailed quickly and father let the engine turn slowly to save fuel. He wanted to try to be in Zutphen before dark in order to anchor there till it turned light again. The rail-way bridge in Zutphen was difficult to clear in the dark. It was starting to get dark when the Orion approached Zutphen. The tower of the St. Walburg church stuck up like a dark finger against the sky.

About a thousand meters upstream from the rail-way bridge the Orion went around and so the bow came to lay against the current. By looking sideways to the shore father could see when the ship would lay still. Jan stood on the bow waiting for a sign from father to show that he could drop the anchor. How cold it was and how long it took before the ship lay still. Finally Jan heard the ship's bell and could drop the anchor. He turned the catcher loose from the winch and with a loud roar of the chain the anchor fell to the bottom of the river.

After supper there was some small talk, but soon mother thought that it was time for Jan and his younger brother to go to bed.

"Jan," father said, "take good care of your brother and when you go to the forecastle don't walk on the hatches because they are slippery with frost."

Together they went to the forecastle and crawled shivering from the cold under the blankets which were covered with hoar-frost. After blowing out their warm breath under the blankets for a while it started to get pleasant and nice and warm and the boys fell asleep.

At one o'clock that night Jan woke up because he heard something. He pricked up his ears and heard oars going through the water. He gave his little brother a poke.

"Wake up! I hear something, listen."

A little later he heard a rowboat push by the Orion and somebody stepped on board. Jan shivered with fright. Meanwhile both of them heard someone coming in the direction of the forecastle. Jan did not have a chance to warn his father, that meant going to the stern and he did not dare go outside. Suddenly they heard someone rattling the handle of the forecastle and trying to come inside. Fortunately the forecastle was locked on the inside. After the man walked around on the deck for a while, he stepped into the rowboat and rowed away. Jan breathed a sigh of relief, crawled far under the blankets and fell asleep.

The Shooting

The Orion was loaded with 250 one-ton bales of sugar on the way from the Somme in Belgium to Roosendaal. Late in the afternoon they arrived in Wemeldinge in front of the locks. Jan was sent on shore to pick up the school children. The plan was to leave early the next morning and with a favorable tide to sail on to Roosendaal. Father went on shore to report to the lock-keeper in order to be able to go through the locks first chance the next morning. In the office of the lock-keeper he also met a German official.

To himself father said, "Now what? Bunch of meddlers!"

After he had reported the measurements and destination of the ship, the lock-keeper said father should be ready the next morning at six o'clock in front of the middle lock. Father thanked him and said he would be ready.

When he wanted to leave he was accosted by the German officer.

"You will not sail by yourself tomorrow. You will sail as the last ship in a convoy," the officer said. "After leaving the locks early in the morning you will wait in the front harbor till you get a signal to start moving. The convoy consists as follows: first a heavily armed patrol boat will leave, then 24 ships of different dimensions and tonnage will follow. Your ship is number 25 and the last one of the convoy. Behind you follows another patrol boat for guarding. Do you understand?"

"Sure," father said, "we'll do our best."

Father took a dim view of the matter and wondered whether everything would work out as that German had said. He knew from experience how difficult it is for individual ships to follow each other. The slowest ship would set the speed and father knew that would be the Orion. On top of that came the fact that it takes a long time to form a convoy and the tide would be gone by then. The Orion had only a small engine capacity and would soon be left behind.

Next morning at five o'clock the alarm clock went off. Through the door of the forecastle in the bow father called, "Jan, get up, we're starting." Yawning, Jan got up and put his clothes on. When he came to the stern, father had already started the engine. There was a lot of bustle in front of the two locks. All the skippers wanted to enter the lock at the same time in order to enter the front harbor as soon as possible so they could go along with the convoy. After half an hour the lock was almost full. The Orion was the last one and with lots of inching and pinching she could just get in.

The lock gates were closed and the water started to rise. After about twenty minutes the lock gates at the other end opened and the ships could leave the lock. The first patrol boat was already floating in the front harbor in expectation of the arrival of the ships. Suddenly a siren screamed from the patrol boat as a signal to 'Follow me.' Then the patrol boat set course for the mouth of the harbor and sailed out. The second patrol boat stayed in the harbor and gave every ship orders as to when it could start sailing and join its predecessor. After about half an hour father heard through the loudspeaker of the patrol boat that the Orion should hurry to join the convoy.

The engine was put on 'ahead' and the Orion sailed out of the harbor. Because all of that had taken quite a bit of time, it was daylight by the time the Orion came out of the harbor. Father looked through the binoculars and saw that the convoy stretched out like a long ribbon between the sandbanks as far as you could see. The convoy had a length of two kilometers or more. The ships had to stay behind each other because in some places the channel was so narrow that two ships could not sail next to each other. Of course, they had to take oncoming ships into account.

After sailing for half an hour father saw that the distance between the Orion and her predecessor kept getting bigger. The commander of the patrol boat noticed this too. The patrol boat turned around and continued sailing a short distance from the Orion. Through the megaphone the commander called to father that he had to sail faster. Father called back that the Orion only had a light engine and that there was only a little amount of fuel in the tanks.

After about ten minutes, the commander had apparently made contact with the other patrol boat, because the ship turned in the direction of the Orion and came alongside at starboard. After the patrol boat was fastened in front and behind, the engine room got the command: 'Full steam ahead.' Well, that was quite noticeable. Slowly the distance between the next to last ship and the Orion got smaller.

On board all vessels a nervous tension reigned, which got worse as the sun rose higher. In the deck-house the mattresses and bedding were put on top of the table again in order to hide under if necessary. Also in the hold a few bags of sugar were removed, so that a deep hole was made. Here the whole family could hide away in a pinch. As well father had made twenty-five wooden pegs to use to close possible bullet holes below the water-line. But so far so good. In the meantime they had passed the harbor of Zijpe and Bruinisse was visible at a distance.

Father was talking with the German commander, a friendly man of about fifty-five. He mentioned that he used to work as head of a drinking water company in the area of Winterberg. He had two growing children he had not seen for eight months. His leaves got scarcer and shorter all the time. He despised Nazi Germany, but was obliged to go into compulsory service. He was glad to be able to stay in Holland and not be directly involved at the front. And he was pleased as commander of a patrol boat to be able to protect Dutch skippers and their families from English air attacks.

On the patrol boat attentiveness prevailed. Two machine-gun nests, each equipped with quadruple quick-firing artillery, were constantly occupied by three soldiers. On deck soldiers with binoculars inspected the horizon. They knew that if airplanes came to attack they would do so with the sun behind them. Because of the brightness of the sun the planes would be noticed late. The sun shone on the convoy from behind. That meant that the Orion would have the first turn. After the noon hour the convoy sailed off the Steenbergsche Vliet in a stretched out ribbon. Many sighed with relief that everything went well so far. A few more hours sailing and then the ships would reach better protected waters. So keep up courage.

But suddenly the quietness was rudely interrupted. On board the patrol boat the sirens howled sadly. All the soldiers came on deck and occupied positions that were appointed beforehand. Everyone looked behind them. Hundreds of meters distant, looking like seagulls just above water level, two planes came in the direction of the convoy. The quick-firing cannons were turned around and pointed in the direction of the airplanes. The commander stood on port-side in the gangway of the patrol boat.

"Look for cover," he called to father. Father jumped into the cockpit of the Orion and called, "Down, under the table." He himself rolled more than walked down the stairs. There was no time to go into the hold.

Jan, however, was curious and did not go down right away. He first wanted to know what was happening. Through the window of the cockpit he looked back and saw at a distance of about one hundred meters behind the Orion and ten meters above the water-line, one of the planes coming straight at them. Suddenly there was a terrible noise on board the patrol boat. All the quick-firing cannons had opened fire on the airplane. He saw beams of white glowing fire heading for the airplane and thought to himself, "That one won't continue for one meter and will crash into the water." To his consternation, however, he saw the plane continue to fly, straight at the Orion. Through the glass dome in the airplane he could see the pilot sitting with his leather cap on his head.

Suddenly, white streams of fire also came from the airplane. Jan rolled down the stairs and crawled on hands and knees under the table with the mattresses. The next moment a hellish cacophony of sounds started up, everywhere was fire and glass. The bullets of the airplane had not only hit the patrol vessel but also the Orion and good too.

When the racket was over, Jan crawled from under the table. He saw that a twenty-one millimeter shell was lying about twenty centimeters from the left leg of his father. The shell had not exploded, that was a miracle. If it had, the consequences would have been incalculable. Cautiously Jan followed his father up the stairs to survey the damage. What they saw was terrible. From the rear machine-gun nest blood streamed down. Two soldiers were dead, the third seriously wounded. In the front machine-gun nest lay a wounded soldier. In the gangway, in the place where shortly before father and the commander stood talking, the commander was lying. Dead. One leg was shot away and large wounds gaped in both his arms and his chest. He must have been killed instantly. Soon after, blood started running down from the patrol boat which lay higher than the Orion. The water was colored red, only the pieces of bone stayed behind in the gangway in contrasting white. The airplanes had pulled up, swerved and left without visible damage. The oldest officer on board the patrol boat took over command.

Together father and Jan went to look at the damage the Orion had sustained during the shooting. In the stern were twelve bullet holes. Some bullet holes at water level. Those holes were closed as well as possible with the wooden pegs that were ready. The glass was cleaned up and the broken windows closed off with plywood. After that the blood of the German sailors was rinsed off the deck.

The journey continued. There was no sign of the convoy. How much damage the other ships sustained was never made known. Later father heard that a cousin sailing in the front of the convoy was killed and his wife seriously wounded. After waiting for several hours in front of the Steenbergsche Vliet till there was enough water, they sailed to Roosendaal, where the Orion was unloaded the next day.

Food Shortages in France

From Roosendaal the empty Orion sailed to Rotterdam. After the damage of the shooting had been fixed as much as possible at the wharf, they loaded up for Lille in Northern France. As everywhere in Europe, food in France was rationed. Every skipper who could prove that his vessel had to load or unload in France was given ration coupons for several days at the border—the passengers of the Orion also. During the journey father and Jan went once in a while on shore to get food. Often that did not work out. Despite the ration coupons many bakers were not in favor of selling their bread to foreigners. They did not even know how to provide enough bread for their own customers. But after a long wait and tramping to many stores Jan usually knew how to worm loose some bread. When that became more difficult and bread still more scarce, Jan used a different technique. He took along his younger brother Wim. If he got a half or a quarter of a loaf of bread this was put in a shopping bag. At the next store Wim had to stay outside and look after the shopping bag.

Milk and meat were very difficult to get. Milk consisted of cans of evaporated milk. They were for sale with coupons but only at the pharmacy. The meat was downright bad. The few times a little was to be had it was tough horse meat or beef with tendons and fat.

Even more difficult to get was soap or powdered detergent. One day mother gave Jan coupons along to buy powdered detergent. In several stores Jan showed his coupons and money. He did not speak enough French to make it understood what he wanted. The shopkeepers noticed and pretended that they did not understand him. So he did not get any. Jan became discouraged. He decided to try one more time. In front of an old-fashioned looking store he stopped and looked through the window. By standing as far as possible to one side of the window he could just look behind and under the counter. And what did he see there? A pile of five boxes of "savon de poudre."

"Now it must go funny," he thought, "if I don't get one of those."

He went into the store and when it was his turn, he showed his coupons and money to the shopkeeper. He tried to ask, in his best French, for a box of powdered detergent.

The shopkeeper put both hands in the air and said, "Non poudre de savon." Jan pointed across the counter to the back of it and said, "Ici, cinq package poudre de savon." The shopkeeper shrugged his shoulders and pretended not to understand.

Jan got angry. He walked around the counter, pulled out a box of powdered detergent and showed it to the shopkeeper. He decided to make the best of it and apparently had a sense of humor. He laughed at Jan, took the coupons and money and said bonjour to Jan. Jan ran out of the store with the powdered detergent. Imagine if the man should change his mind. At a trot he went to the ship and full of pride showed his booty to his mother.

"How did you get that?" she asked.

"Well, if you know the way and speak the language some, you manage," he boasted.

To Germany

In Nancy, on the French river Meuse, the Orion loaded iron ore for a German steel factory in the Ruhr.

"How could you do that?" mother said to father when he returned on board. "You know how dangerous it is there. Besides Ina and Jan we have four more little children on board, of which Jaap is only a few months old. Every night the British air force carries out bombings. They don't see any difference between a Dutch or a German ship."

"There is no other work to be had," father said, "and there has to be bread on the table."

The Orion left and sailed that week to Weurt via Nijmegen. There Sunday was kept first. Father did not want to sail on Sunday unless there was no other possibility.

Monday morning the engine was started early and the hard trip to Germany was begun. At a speed of three to four kilometers an hour the Orion sailed up the Rhine. In the afternoon they came to Lobith-Tolkamer and the ship was cleared by Dutch customs. While leaving the ship the oldest customs officer said, without his colleague hearing it, "Skipper, I hope you'll get back in one piece because in the Ruhr they get a spanking almost every night."

"Thank you," father said.

After lifting the anchor the Orion sailed over the border to Emmerik. There, however, things did not go so pleasantly. A patrol boat of the German Customs flew towards the Orion at high speed and someone barked through the megaphone: "Dock alongside the ships in the third row up, nobody is allowed off the ship." Father stuck his hand out the door of the cockpit to signal that he had understood.

The Orion sailed to the appointed spot. Jan let the front anchor down and secured a cable to the vessel they had to dock next to.

"A dangerous place to be," Jan heard his father say to mother. "With so many ships together it is a cinch for the English planes to hit the mark."

After waiting for three quarters of an hour a patrol boat appeared out of nowhere. Three men in uniform with huge caps and pistols in their belts jumped on board the Orion. One of them walked to the bow to inspect the forecastle. The other two walked to the stern and went into the deck-house without asking. After taking a chair, the oldest of the two asked for the list of the crew, passports and the grocery list (all the food was listed on this.)

In the meantime number two got up and inspected the kitchen. He looked in all the canisters, filled with foodstuffs such as sugar, salt and rice and shook them to see if there was something in the bottom. With the aid of the provision list he checked the amount. All the cupboards were turned upside down and spaces that sounded hollow when he hit them had to be opened up. Mother watched with gnashing teeth but could not say anything. Nothing was found that would not pass.

In the meantime the passports were checked and stamped. The provision list was also stamped. The oldest official informed father that the papers were in order and that he could go on shore to the shipping agent for clearance. When the other official was finished with the inspection of the kitchen, he wanted to enter the deck-house. However, he stood as nailed to the floor in the door opening. He looked hard at the back wall of the deck-house where a large photograph was hanging of Queen Emma, in state robes.

His face turned bright red and he burst loose in German. It was scandalous that somebody had the nerve to hang up a photo of a Dutch Queen instead of a photo of Hitler and dare sail into the Great Germany with it. Mother was watching while wringing her hands. How would this end? On the outside father stayed calm. Because of the many years he had sailed into Germany he could understand and speak the German language quite well.

"That photo has been hanging there for years," father said. "We sailed over the border with it several times and nothing was ever said about it."

The official burst out anew. That was none of his business. He would arrest father and take him on shore he said.

The older official, who apparently had a higher rank, was getting tired of the behavior of his colleague. He gave him the order to keep his mouth shut. The younger official clicked his heels, saluted and stood still. The older man asked father how long the photo had been on board.

"We had this ship built in 1927," father said, "and we got the picture then from the shipyard. I never thought about putting it away, but if you think it is necessary you can take it."

Father thought about other things on board that even mother did not know about. He wanted to avoid any further searching.

"I will take it," the official said, "and keep it to a warning this time."

The officials left the ship. Father was picked up by a boat that took him to shore to get clearance from the shipping agent. After two hours father was ready and was brought back to the ship.

"Where have you been all this time?" mother lashed out. "I thought those villains had arrested you after all."

"Oh no," father said, "but there are more ships and then it takes a long time. But everything is ready. We have to wait for the customs officers now to seal the hold."

Around five o'clock that afternoon a customs vessel came alongside on which was written in big letters 'Zoll.' Two officers stepped on board the Orion and inspected first the customs seals of the Dutch customs. Then the hold was opened and the load inspected. Everything seemed to be in order. Father and Jan got the order to close the hold again and put the sealing wax on. The officials attached the seal and stamped the papers belonging to the load. Then they told us we could continue our journey. They left the ship. The mooring cables were thrown loose and the anchor pulled up, after which the journey was continued.

In the meantime it had turned seven o'clock that night and soon it would be dark.

"It would be best to continue to Spijk," father said, "and spend the night there. We must stay a long way away from the cattle feed factory. Imagine the English getting it into their head to bomb the factory tonight, then we won't be very comfortable so close by."

After sailing for an hour and a half they arrived and stopped to spend the night there. It was just as well they did not know what was in store for them.

After supper it was soon bedtime. When Jan walked to the bow to go to sleep he heard high in the sky a heavy droning sound. He walked back to the stern and called for father.

"What is that racket in the sky?" he asked.

Father came on deck and listened.

"Those are passing planes," he said, "on their way to the Ruhr. Fortunately we won't have any trouble with them here."

Satisfied Jan went to the bow and crawled into bed. That night there was a full moon and a clear sky. Through the porthole in the forecastle Jan could see the stars from his bed. Tired from his long day he fell asleep.

After several hours he awoke from a lot of noise.

"What's going on?" he asked himself.

Quickly he pulled on a pair of pants and a jacket and went on deck. When he looked in the direction of the factory he saw a big cloud of smoke against the clear sky. He also saw enormous search-lights that searched the sky for airplanes. Suddenly he saw an airplane appear in the light of one of the search-lights. It shone like silver. At the same time a few more light-beams were added and it looked like the plane was caught in a web.

Shortly after that heavy artillery came into action. Around the airplane dozens of little puffs of smoke could be seen from the exploding shells. They looked like mushrooms. The airplane however quietly continued and did not seem to take any notice of the guns. After a while the search-lights could not reach it anymore and it disappeared from the light-beams. The search-lights went out and everything was quiet again. The sky stayed colored for a long time because of the fires. But this too got slowly less as the fires were brought under control.

"Jan, quickly go to bed," father said, "you can still sleep for a few hours before we sail. Who knows what's waiting for us tomorrow night."

"Yes, I will," Jan said, "goodnight."

It seemed like he had only just gone to bed when he heard father call through the forecastle: "Jan get up, we're going to sail." While mother took the helm Jan and father pulled the anchor in. And that woke Jan up very well.

After they had been sailing for several hours father looked behind him down the river for the umpteenth time. He got a big scare.

"Mother, take the helm," he called downstairs.

Mother did not know what was happening and ran up the stairs into the cockpit in a fright. Jan just came out of the engine room and also stepped into the cockpit. He heard father say, "The Germans are coming, take the helm and sail straight ahead." He quickly took a screwdriver and went into the bathroom. After five minutes father came back and took the helm again. Jan saw that behind the Orion a fast patrol boat sailed in a zigzag course, so that it could see both sides of the Orion regularly.

Soon after it came alongside the Orion and five customs officials in black uniforms jumped on board. The patrol boat went back to sailing behind the Orion again, so that nothing could be thrown overboard without it being noticed. Two officials, equipped with flashlights and sticks with a little mirror on the end, went to the bow. The other three stepped into the cockpit.

The oldest talked to father and said that they were customs officials and wanted to have an after-check. Two of them had in the meantime gone down the stairs to the deck-house. The oldest official asked father for the passports and crew list.

"I'll go and get them," father said.

"Take the helm, Jan." And softly he added, "now it is hearing, seeing, and mouth shut, if you know what I mean."

Well, Jan knew very well. His knees were knocking together. Father came back with the papers and handed them to the official. He carefully looked through them and said, "Everything is in order."

"Thank you," father said.

He noticed that the screwdriver was still in his pants pocket. He took it out and put it in its place. Meanwhile the other two in the deck-house made a big mess. Everything was turned upside down. Even the mattresses were taken out of the berths, cut open and inspected. Also the bottoms of the berths were removed to see what was underneath.

One of them meanwhile started to inspect the bathroom. He called a colleague and asked for a screwdriver.

"I believe a tile in the wall is loose," he said.

After loosening a wood screw and removing the tile, a space became visible of the size of a cigar box. He turned on his flashlight and shone it into the space. The space was empty, there was nothing in it.

Father was called and Jan took the helm. Father was asked with a snarl what the space was for.

"Oh," father said, "when we make a long trip to France I keep my cigars in there, they keep better at the right temperature."

The officials looked at each other and felt they were made fun of. After the inspection was finished they went back on board the patrol boat and sailed away. The Orion could also continue on her way.

Jan asked father why he had to go to the bathroom in such a hurry when he saw the Germans come up from behind.

"Did you get a belly-ache?" he asked.

"Indeed," father said, "I got a pain in my belly when I saw them coming up behind. Because you know, that empty space they came across in the bathroom had a pistol in it a little earlier. I threw it through the porthole into the river, fortunately at the moment when the patrol boat sailed on the other side of the Orion. I have had that pistol on board for years without anybody knowing about it. Not even your mother. Fortunately I've never had to use it. If the Germans had found the pistol I would not be standing here now. Luckily everything worked out well.

"You know," father said, "one of those guys was the man who came on board at the German border and took the photograph of Queen Emma along then. His superior prevented my coming along as well. Since he couldn't get his way he tried it in this manner."

Jan blushed with excitement at his smart father.

The Ruhr

After sailing for two days the Orion drew near to the Ruhr. A fearful mood reigned. There was much traffic on the river, especially the many government vessels that sailed to and fro. On both sides of the river a large number of balloons floated. They were supposed to keep the English airplanes at a high altitude. Well, the English did that anyway. During the nightly raids with hundreds of airplanes participating they had to fly high in order not to be in each others' way and get hit.

A patrol vessel of the Polizei came alongside the Orion. The official stepped on board and asked father where the Orion was going.

"To the harbor of Rheinstahl," father said.

"May I see your papers for a minute?" he asked. After checking them he said: "All in order—they are expecting you. It is the third harbor on the port side of the river. You have to unload at the high wharf at the back of the harbor."

After sailing for half an hour they came to the harbor. Because the water in the river was very low, the mouth of the harbor was very narrow. Father steered the Orion into the harbor while Jan kept a look-out on the forward deck to see if any ships wanted to sail out of the harbor. On both sides along the riverbanks lay many empty ships. The banks were messy and dirty. They were covered with a thick layer of brown dust coming from the steel factories. Heavy clouds of smoke hung over the harbor and the smell was unbearable. At the back of the harbor was a high wharf. But because of the low water this looked even higher than usual. There was not one ship. Jan thought it strange.

He would soon discover the reason for this. The Orion was moored at the high wharf and father went on shore to report his arrival. A little later a man appeared on the wharf eight meters above who called to Jan: "Open the hatches, we'll start unloading right away." Jan raised his hand as a sign that he had understood.

He said to mother: "The seals are still on it, can I take those off without customs being here?"

"I wouldn't do that," mother said. "Wait till father gets back."

That turned out to be a wise decision, because a little later father came back with a customs official.

After descending the steep ladder in the wall of the wharf, the seals were carefully inspected. They were found to be in order and they were allowed to open the hatches. A little later a crane floated above the hold and the first ore was unloaded. Meanwhile three shabbily dressed men appeared on the wharf, who descended the ladder on the wharf and climbed into the hold. They were badly dressed and very skinny. Their eyes lay deeply in their sockets. After that a fourth man appeared on the wharf. He also climbed down. He was a German soldier who had to guard the men in the hold. They turned out to be prisoners. He carried a gun over his shoulder and stood in the gangway. The prisoners had to shovel the ore to the center of the hold, so the crane could get at it better.

"Who are those men?" Jan asked.

"Those are prisoners of the Germans, they probably came from Poland or the Balkans," father said. "They have a very bad time here, the Germans hate them."

As was her custom mother had brewed coffee in the meantime. The men in the hold were included as well. When mother came on deck with a serving tray with full coffee cups and held it in front of the soldier he took a cup. When she wanted to give it to the men in the hold the soldier objected. They were prisoners and did not need coffee. Jan was furious: "The bugger, he guzzled the coffee himself, but those poor beggars who need it a lot more weren't allowed to have any."

After about two hundred tons were unloaded it was time to stop. It was six o'clock by now, the prisoners went to their huts and the soldier to the barracks.

The foreman called to father that they would continue next morning at seven o'clock. Exhausted the men climbed from the hold up to the wharf. In the meantime mother had dinner ready and called father and Jan. After washing and changing into clean clothes they sat down at the table, where all the little ones were waiting impatiently.

The Air Raid

That first evening in the Ruhr they had hardly laid down in bed when the sirens started to wail as a signal of an air raid alarm. Quickly father and mother discussed whether to stay on board and wait and see what would happen or if they should go on shore to find an bomb shelter. Father thought it irresponsible to stay on board ship. Quickly everyone was dressed. A suitcase with clothes for the youngest children was packed and they went on deck. But then the problems started. How could they quickly get up those steep stairs? Eight meters high and the children drunk with sleep. How would that go?

"You go first Jan," father said, "then I'll bring the children. You take them at the edge of the wharf and watch them till we're all there."

And that's how it happened. Jan was waiting when father came with the first child. It was pitch black. Only after a long time of getting used to it could you see something.

Ina came first, she could climb by herself. After a few minutes Jan heard his father say: "Jan are you there? Grab this one." Shortly after Jan grabbed his younger brother and put him on one of the rail-way tracks.

"Don't stand up," Jan said, "sit there till I come back."

The first four children were taken up by father. They put their arms around father's neck and their legs around his waist. Jan put them all in a row on the tracks.

"As long as the train doesn't come," Jan thought.

They were waiting now for the youngest brother, Jaap. He was not one year old yet and could not hold on to father. But father could not hold on to him and climb the ladder, now what? Time was pressing, the bombers were coming closer all the time and the bomb shelters would be closed.

"Hold him for a minute," father said to mother who stood with Jaap in the gangway. Quickly he went back and got the big tin tub from the quarter-deck. He put his coat on the bottom and walked to the bow to get a rope. The rope he tied to both handles of the tub and with the other end he walked up the ladder.

"Here Jan," father said, "grab this. When I call you have to pull."

Shortly after Jan heard his father call: "Pull Jan!" Jan started pulling but had no idea what was going on. In the meantime mother had laid Jaap in the tub. Father walked up the ladder as closely as possible to the tub. Sitting on the edge of the wharf Jan saw the tub appearing.

"Now what's up?" he thought. Soon after he saw Jaap lying in the tub. "If only this will work out all right," he thought. "If the tub tilts a little he will fall out."

Fortunately everything went fine.

"I'm going back one more time," father said to Jan, "to get mother and the suitcase."

And soon mother as well as the suitcase were on the wharf.

"Now look for a bomb shelter," father said.

About one hundred meters away from them mother saw a dim light burning. She also saw silhouettes walking in the direction of the light.

"That must be a bomb shelter."

"I think so too," father said.

They all quickly walked in a row, one behind the other on the rail-way tracks, there seemed to be no end to them. Father carried Piet and mother carried Jaap. The other children had to walk themselves. Once in a while one of the children tripped and hurt a knee, but finally they all arrived safely at the bomb shelter.

When they had approached within a few meters of the bomb shelter, father heard a woman's voice on the inside of the door saying, "Move along, the door is closing."

"Wait a minute," father called, "we want to get in too."

The woman stuck her head out, but could not see anything in the dark.

She called: "Anybody there?"

"Yes, yes," father called, "wait with closing the door."

"Hurry up," the woman said, "I can hear the airplanes already."

Panting because of the running, the family went into the bomb shelter. The heavy door fell shut behind them and was locked. For a moment Jan thought it a scary idea. Shut in, without knowing what would happen. The guard came into the waiting area. Through an open door you could see hospital beds. Everyone sat nicely on the benches along the sides. Jaap lay on mother's lap. The other children pushed close against her, scared of the unknown and the strange children around them.

The guard looked around and saw a German woman with a shopping bag on her lap with the zipper open a little bit.

Suspicious from experience he kept an eye on the bag. Sure enough, suddenly she saw the bag move a little bit. She rushed to the woman and snapped: "What's in that bag?"

"Clothing," the woman answered.

"Let me see," the guard said.

"No," was the answer, "there is no need."

"I want to see what's in that bag," the guard barked, "I am boss here." She grabbed the bag, pulled it towards her and looked inside. In the bag she saw a little shivering dog with two beady eyes.

"You know animals are not allowed in the bomb shelter," the guard said. "They use too much oxygen that we may badly need ourselves yet. You can choose, the dog out of the bomb shelter, then you can stay or both of you go!"

"Then I go too," the woman said. She stood up and walked to the door. The guard opened the door and the woman walked into the night with her little dog. The door closed behind her.

Shortly after the bombing started. The bomb shelter rattled and shook. Sometimes Jan had the feeling that the bomb shelter was lifted up and flung back down again. The overhead lighting was changed to emergency lighting, fed by some batteries.

The airplanes flew in groups. As a result there regularly was a short pause between the exploding bombs. During these pauses a tense silence reigned in the bomb shelter and everyone waited for the next wave of attack. During one of these pauses all those present heard from the back of the bomb shelter a child's voice call out: "Agnes, he pooped." Everyone sat up and laughed. When Jan looked in the direction of the sound he saw a young mother who was sitting down with two little children. A baby lay on her lap and a girl of about five sat next to her. But the incident had temporarily broken the tension. A little later the next wave of attack started. In between the exploding bombs you could hear the anti-aircraft guns shooting at the airplanes.

After about an hour it got quiet. The bomb shelter however stayed locked until a signal from outside was given that everything was safe. After waiting a while, it was now five o'clock in the morning, the guard got a signal that everything was safe and the door could be opened.

Nervously everyone went outside. What would they find? When Jan came outside he saw that the sky was red from the burning fires, it looked like the whole world was on fire. Father was not sure what to do. Go back to the ship or stay on shore. You never knew when another alarm would come. He asked the guard if he could stay in the bomb shelter a little longer with the family. But that was not allowed. The shelter could only be used when there was an alarm.

"Come, mother," father said, "then we'll go back to the Orion and wait and see. We can't stay here in the open air with the children."

But the way back was more difficult than the way there. The terrain was riddled with large bomb craters. In some places pieces of railroad track stuck up in the air like macabre figures.

After a difficult trip they got back to the wharf where the Orion had been left. Father looked anxiously over the edge of the wharf wall. To his great relief the Orion lay just as he had left her. Carefully mother went on board first. After that the bigger children who could walk by themselves were helped on board ship by father. Lastly Jaap, the baby, had to be brought back on board.

"Wait there," father called to Jan, "I'll come up to see if the rope is tied well to the tub." But Jan could not see a tub anywhere. When father came up on the wharf Jan said: "The tub is gone."

"What now?" father said, "we can't do without. Stay with the baby while I go and look."

About fifty meters from the place where they had left it, between bomb craters and bent rails, father found the tub again. Except for a few dents it was not damaged. The rope was still in one piece too. The baby was laid in the tub and put on the edge of the wharf.

"I'll stand on the stairs," father said to Jan, "and you keep the rope taut till I say you can pay it out."

After five minutes the baby was on board ship as well and was put to bed right away. "Try to sleep for a while," father said to mother and the children, "I'll stay up, you never know."

Nothing else happened that night however. At seven o'clock the prisoners came in the hold again and the guard stood in the gangway. Unloading started right away. When the Orion was empty in the afternoon father said "We're leaving here. That high wall is too dangerous to get off the ship. Look Jan, that's why all those empty ships are in the front of the harbor. There it is much easier and faster to get off the ship if necessary."

After the Orion was moored in a better place everyone went early to bed very tired. That night it stayed quiet.

Loading for IJmuiden

The next morning at nine o'clock a military car stopped in front of the Orion and a soldier came on board. Jan was busy cleaning the ship. The soldier called Jan and asked if father was on board. Jan went to get him and shortly after father came on deck from the deck-house. He asked the soldier what he wanted.

"The senior officer wants to speak to you," the soldier said. "You can ride along with me, I'll take you there."

"OK," father said, "I'll change my clothes." He quickly put on a clean shirt, a different pair of pants and shoes. He put the ship's papers in his jacket pocket and went with the soldier. The Senior officer received father kindly, shook his hand and said: "Sit down." He told him he had been informed that the Orion was empty and wanted to leave for Holland. "I need a ship like that to load steel plates of 20 meters by 4.20 meters for IJmuiden. Will you do that voluntarily? If not, I'll have to confiscate your ship and put a soldier on guard. However, I'd rather not do that."

Father said, "I have my family on board with small children and don't feel safe here. Last night we had to flee to a bomb shelter. I want to go to Holland as soon as possible. But I understand I have no choice."

"Indeed," the senior officer said, "you have to load here."

"Then I have one request," father said, "please arrange that I can load and leave as soon as possible."

"I'll have that taken care of for you," the commander said, "and I'll issue you some extra fuel as well. Wait a moment."

The senior officer took the phone off the hook and a little later an officer of lower rank came in and saluted.

"Mister Muller," the commander said, "this skipper will load his ship in the Walsum harbor with steel plates for IJmuiden. Take care of the paperwork and arrange for a tugboat to take the ship there and give him an extra allotment of fuel to sail to Holland. Notify the factory that loading has to start immediately and that the ship will be finished right away."

"Yes, sir," the officer said. He saluted and left.

"Everything is in order," the senior officer said, "you can go to your ship and make sure you're ready to sail."

"It will be taken care of, sir," father said, "I thank you for your cooperation."

"You are welcome," the man said, "I have children myself, I hope our children will survive this cursed war. Auf wiedersehn."

"Well," father thought, "he's probably no friend of Hitler." He went outside and was taken to the Orion again by the soldier with the car.

Mother was glad when she saw father step on board again.

"You never know what those Germans are up to."

Jan was working in the bow when he saw the car arriving. He ran back to hear what father had to say.

"And how did it go?" mother asked father as he stepped into the cockpit.

"Well," father said, "I was taken to the senior officer and he knew that our ship was unloaded. But he also knew that we have one hold and can take long plates. A ship with such a long hold is not available in this area at this time. So he asked if we wanted to load steel plates for IJmuiden. He also said there was no choice and that he would coerce us otherwise. We'll get some extra fuel for the engine. I'll change first. Jan you make the ship ready to sail, any moment now a tugboat will come to take us to our loading-berth."

While father was changing a heavy tugboat came alongside. The captain showed father a paper that said he had to take the Orion to the Walsum harbor.

"We'll sail about three hours upstream before we get there. We'll pull your ship with a cross-wire so you won't have to steer," he said.

"OK," father said, "we're ready to go."

The tugboat left with the Orion for her loading-berth. The ship had never in her whole existence sailed as fast as that afternoon. At six o'clock they sailed into the harbor where they had to load and the Orion was moored underneath a huge crane.

Father went on shore with the papers to report himself ready to load. The wharfinger told him to open up the whole ship so loading could be started at seven o'clock the next morning. They would load continually until the ship was loaded. The night passed quietly. The next morning at the stroke of seven they did start. First, four prisoners of war came on board who had to lay the steel plates in the right spot in the hold. In between the steel plates in different spots a small wooden beam was placed. This way a space was left to be able to attach the chains, but this also prevented the plates from sliding over each other.

Jan could see the men laboring in the hold. They were as thin as kindling and had difficulty keeping on their feet. They were very undernourished. The soldier who kept watch over the prisoners was an older man who did not seem to care by the looks of it.

"Would you like a cup of coffee in the cockpit?" father asked the soldier.

"Gladly," he said, "because it's cold when you stand still."

When the soldier stepped inside the cockpit on one side, Jan left the cockpit on the other side with a jug of coffee and four cups. Without anybody noticing he gave the jug of coffee and the cups to the prisoners in the hold. They hardly took the time to pour the coffee. They slurped it up.

"Good job," Jan thought, "that the coffee isn't boiling hot, otherwise they would have burned themselves."

The jug was put out of sight in a corner of the hold so they would have some more to drink later. Meanwhile the loading continued. From the soldier father had heard that the prisoners were Russian soldiers who were treated badly.

"Do you know how many potatoes are left in the forecastle?" mother asked Jan at one time.

"Sure," Jan said. He had to get the potatoes every day after all. "Another five or six meals," he said.

"Great," mother said, "here is a bucket and get eight more potatoes than usual."

"Whatever that was necessary for?" Jan thought, but he would wait and see.

Mother peeled the potatoes and boiled them. From father she found out if the prisoners would go on shore to eat at noon.

"No," father said. "The soldier told me that they'll have to continue working until the ship is loaded and ready to leave."

"Good," mother said, "will you ask the soldier if it is all right if we give the people in the hold something to eat too? Father spoke to the soldier about it.

"Not really," the soldier said, "but I have no eyes in the back of my head. If you give me a signal I'll walk to the front of the ship and you can give them something to eat."

Father gave the soldier a signal and he did what he had said. Meanwhile mother had given Jan a dish with eight big potatoes with gravy.

"Give this dish to the people in the hold," she said, "but make sure it won't be noticed on shore."

"I will," Jan said.

He whistled between his teeth to the prisoners and unseen he gave the dish with potatoes to one of them. In an unintelligible language they thanked him. They quickly crawled in a corner of the hold and snatched the potatoes out of the dish with their fingers and shoved them into their mouths. In a moment the dish was empty and they gave it back to Jan. Once again a number of unintelligible sounds were uttered.

By two o'clock that afternoon three quarters of the load was stowed in the hold and the prisoners were allowed on shore one by one for a visit to the washroom. The washroom was located in a hut, close to the ship, where the prisoners were housed. When number four returned, he carried a parcel wrapped in newspaper under his arm. After he returned on board the Orion he called Jan and handed over the parcel. Jan blushed. "Such poor devils and still give something away?"

Jan quickly went into the deck-house to open the parcel. What he found surpassed his expectations. It was a hand-crafted peacock made of wood. It had a handle and two little wheels. Jan put it on the floor and pushed the bird back and forth. The movement caused the wings to move up and down and it looked like the bird wanted to fly. The peacock was painted in beautiful bright colors. Mother clapped her hands together in amazement,

"That is beautiful. How can such poor devils make something so beautiful?" she wondered. Unfortunately the bird was burned at the end of the war.

By six o'clock that evening the last steel plate came into the hold. The prisoners were commanded to go on shore. While they were standing at the bottom of the stairs mother came outside and threw a whole loaf of bread into the hold. Dexterously it was caught. While fearfully looking around the bread was divided into quarters and hidden under their clothes. The soldier acted as if he did not notice anything. Because it had gotten too late in the meantime to sail, the Orion stayed at the wharf. Fortunately this wharf was noticeably lower than the wharf where they had docked three nights ago. The hold was closed and the deck rinsed off. Meanwhile mother had put bread on the table and they ate.

At ten o'clock that night the misery started again. The children were just in bed and father and mother made ready to go when the sirens started howling. They were however better prepared now. The clothes were ready and the suitcase packed. Within five minutes the whole family stood on the wharf.

"This way," father called while carrying the baby in his arms. "This afternoon I saw that there is a bomb shelter here."

They were barely in the bomb shelter when the bomb shower started. It seemed like a hailstorm. Every so often a carpet of bombs was laid close by, then far away. Only by morning did it let up. After father took mother and the children back on board ship he commanded Jan to stay on board to watch. He wanted to find out if any of the Dutch ships at the back of the harbor had been hit. When he came back half an hour later he looked dejected.

"They used pressurized torpedoes last night," he recounted. "Those things spread an enormous air pressure. Kill people, but do little other damage. I heard that a Dutch family stayed on board instead of going to the bomb shelter. Apparently the skipper went on deck during the bombing and was hit by the air pressure of a torpedo. His remains were found in the mast when it got light—horrible."

Firebombs

In the summer of 1943 the Orion loaded artificial fertilizer in Stein (Limburg) for the city of Groningen. The trip went quite well for that time. Except that during the crossing of the IJsselmeer, from Kampen to Lemmer, a German patrol boat came alongside. The captain told father that the night before an Allied plane, on the way back from a mission to Germany, had crashed in the IJsselmeer. The machine had not been located yet. If anything was found or if an oil slick was noticed father had to report that to the Germans on the lock at Lemmer. We saw nothing however.

After the artificial fertilizer was unloaded and the hold scrubbed another load had to be found. In Groningen nothing was available to be shipped. But a skipper had said to father, "If you don't succeed in Groningen try in Delfzijl. The Germans import much lumber from overseas for their defenses. If it works out, an oceangoing vessel will come to unload in Delfzijl."

The next day father went in his good suit to Delfzijl by train. On Tuesday he registered himself at the shipping-exchange. There he was told that the next Saturday an oceangoing vessel with lumber was expected. A part of the load had to be transported in a large inland vessel with a long hold. That was an opportunity. An agreement was written up and a contract signed. They would load as much as the Orion could hold.

"If I may give you some good advice," the charterer said to father, "then take a few buckets of sand on board. Could come in handy."

"Why sand?" father wondered, "we don't have a cat on board."

"Can you be ready for loading in the outer harbor of Delfzijl this coming Monday?" the charterer asked.

"That will be fine," father said.

Cheerfully he left the office and returned to Groningen. On board the Orion everybody was glad that work had been found so quickly and that they did not have to sail to Holland with an empty ship. Without hurry they sailed to Delfzijl. On Saturday morning they docked in the outer harbor and had to wait until Monday morning before they could load.

Sometime on Sunday a freighter sailed into the harbor. It had a large deck-cargo of lumber on board. The ship was moored to some buoys that were anchored in the middle of the harbor. Father looked through the binoculars to read the name of the ship.

"Yes sir, that's her," he said to Jan. "Tomorrow morning at seven o'clock we have to be alongside of her to load. I hope it will go quickly, because in the middle of the harbor like that you are nicely in view of the English fighter planes."

Early on Monday morning they started. The Orion was docked alongside the freighter. The hatches were opened and the ship was ready for loading. Then a tugboat appeared alongside the freighter to put dock-workers on board. The loading-cranes had been made ready by the crew and the engineer had made sure there was plenty of power for the winches.

"There," father said, "now I'm first going to light a pipe."

He took his tobacco box and realized that it was empty. He went to the deck-house and filled it up. Next he filled his pipe. After blowing a few big clouds of smoke the tobacco was pushed smooth in the pipe with the back of the matchbox. He stood up from the table, put the tobacco box in his pants pocket and went up on deck. Mother, Ina and most of the little children stayed in the deck-house. When father stepped out of the cockpit at the side of the big freighter, he heard a loud splash between the freighter and the Orion. He looked over the railing and saw with great alarm that one of the little children lay in the water. He never thought twice but jumped fully clothed from the empty ship into the water next to the little one. The little boy immediately grabbed father and tried to climb onto his shoulders to get out of the water. But then a big problem presented itself— father could not swim. While treading water and looking for support between the two vessels he tried to keep himself and the child above water. Meanwhile he called for help.

But his cries for help were not heard by anybody. Mother and the children were in the cockpit. And on the freighter his cries were drowned out by hissing steam and yelling men's voices. And he got so tired, how much longer could he keep this up? After five minutes mother missed one of the smallest children in the cockpit. She went up the stairs to the deck-house to see if maybe he was up there. But once upstairs she did not see anyone. Neither was father to be seen anywhere on the ship. Fear gripped her heart. She stepped out of the deck-house and went to look on deck.

While she looked around she heard through all the noises a weak call for help. She walked to the railing and looked beside the ship in the water. She changed color. She saw father and the little boy in the water between the ships. She screamed for help. Yes, she was heard on the freighter. A few men looked over the bulwarks and saw father in the water with the child. In a flash a rope was thrown and with one hand on the rope and one hand on the child father was then able to keep his head above water. Then rescue work was quickly started and father and the little one were deposited on deck of the Orion.

After father changed into dry clothes and caught his breath he took his tobacco box to fill his pipe. The well-sealed box had however filled with water. That is how long father and the little one had been in the water.

In spite of all the trouble a start was made with loading. One bundle of lumber after another was taken on board the Orion. When loading was stopped that Monday evening about three quarters of the load was on board the Orion and the lumber was already visible above the spar. Meanwhile that day a lot of smaller ships were loaded as well. They were not allowed to leave yet and had to stay alongside the freighter until the next morning. First the German customs officers had to inspect.

Father went to take a look on board the freighter. He saw that the crew was busy placing buckets of sand in different areas on the wood. "What could that be for?" he thought to himself. Suddenly he saw the light.

Fortunately he himself had also placed four buckets of sand on board the Orion without knowing what they were for. Father went back to his own ship. Together with Jan he took out the buckets of sand and placed them in different places on the lumber as he had seen on the oceangoing ship earlier. While father and Jan stood looking out over the quiet harbor for a moment they heard a small plane. When they looked up they saw a reconnaissance plane fly in circles over the harbor and swerve in a westerly direction shortly after. Father nervously pulled on his pipe.

They went into the deck-house to eat.

"Mother," father said, "you may as well put the little ones to bed early and let them leave their clothes on. It could be a long, warm night."

Mother got a scare. "What do you mean by that?" she asked.

"Well," father said, "when I see what preparations were made on the freighter I don't know what is going to happen. Wait and see."

At ten o'clock that evening father and mother were just going to go to bed, when they heard the sirens in Delfzijl go off for an air raid alarm. This was followed directly by an alarm on the freighter. The crew quickly spread out over the ship and took their appointed places. Mother woke Ina and Jan and said that they should quickly get dressed because there was an air raid alarm. The little ones she left a little longer. A small suitcase with ship's documents and a few articles of clothing for the children she took to the cockpit. If the ship had to be evacuated it would be easy to take in the rowboat. After the sirens stopped a time of ominous silence followed.

Suddenly this was shattered by the sound of approaching airplanes. At the same time the anti-aircraft guns around Delfzijl started spitting fire. Two of the three airplanes flew at low height over the harbor and the ships in it. But to everyone's amazement the airplanes did not shoot or bomb. Shortly after the airplanes left the sky turned a rosy-red color. Now here and now there sharply lit up. Also on the freighter next to the Orion everything was lit up. It looked like daylight.

"Firebombs," father called, "everyone stay inside, I'll go and see if any fell on board here." Fortunately he did not see any.

After father returned to the cockpit the anti-aircraft guns started again. A little later the airplanes came flying over the harbor again, but at greater height this time in order not to be seen in the light caused by themselves. This time however, they could see their targets clearly.

Several fires either had not been extinguished yet or had blazed up again. Especially on board the smaller ships, where no precautions had been made, the fire quickly blazed up again. Suddenly it rained firebombs again. The freighter got several on board and the Orion did not escape either this time. Three firebombs stayed on the deck-cargo of lumber, ignited soon after, and spread a fierce glow. Father ran outside, grabbed a broom and was able to shove a bomb overboard with one push before it got too hot to come close. A second bomb was buried with sand from one of the buckets that was standing ready and was extinguished that way.

The third bomb started burning more and more brightly and gave off enormous heat. By kneeling down father was able to avoid most of the heat. Every time he got close to the bomb with the broom he held his breath as long as possible in order not to breath in any harmful vapors. He quickly gave the bomb a push toward the edge of the deck-cargo. On the rough wood the bomb would not easily roll. But after several tries the bomb did roll over the edge of the deck-cargo, fell into the water and went under with a loud hiss. A sigh of relief escaped father.

After everything got quiet again father and Jan went on the deck-cargo to render the third bomb harmless. With a shovel the sand was thrown aside and the bomb appeared. It looked like a round piece of wood of about half a meter long and five centimeters in diameter. While father and Jan were looking at the bomb, blue-green flames appeared in several places on and around the bomb that quickly got bigger.

"Quickly cover it with sand, Jan," father said, "it is a phosphorous bomb. Every time it is out in the open air and gets oxygen it starts burning again."

Father took the shovel from Jan. Next he threw the bomb with sand and all into the water. "There, that won't bother us anymore," father said.

Meanwhile it was already two o'clock in the morning. Most fires were extinguished.

"It is quiet now," father said, "we better go to sleep for a few hours."

At seven o'clock loading was started again. At twelve o'clock that afternoon the Orion was filled.

"Now we hope the customs officers will come quickly," father said, "then we can at least get away from here before night. In the lock in Delfzijl we will surely lay quieter."

Fortunately that was the case. At two o'clock that afternoon a customs officer came on board. He handed the necessary papers over to father and said that the Orion could leave. That did not fall on deaf ears. Quickly the mooring cables were thrown off and the engine started. The lock-crew had already noticed the coming of the Orion. After a short wait the lock-gates were opened and the Orion could sail into the lock. That night the Orion lay quietly within the locks. But in the harbor of Delfzijl there was heavier fighting that night than the night before. Again the sky was colored red by the flames far and around.

Going Underground

The longer the war lasted the fiercer Hitler and his cronies became. Motor-vessels such as the Orion and Kempenaars were confiscated by the dozen. They were taken to a shipyard to be "beheaded." The bow was partially removed and instead a landing-hatch was installed. That way a hold was created where motorized war material could be parked. In the Netherlands and Belgium the ships would be loaded and then sail to England while joined two by two. There on the beaches the moving materials would be unloaded. That way Germany wanted to occupy England as well.

Besides that there was the increasing danger of being shot at from the air. The English fighter planes showed themselves deeper and deeper in the hinterland. Not only Germans, but also many Dutchmen perished because of these attacks. Because of the enormous losses of the Germans in Europe and South-Africa they had to divide their arms among several fronts. The Allied armies however received more and more weapons because of increased production of war material in England and especially America.

One day Jan heard father and mother talking together about the continuing war. Father said it could not last much longer. The German losses were enormous, especially at the Eastern front. But with a family on board we were vulnerable. We must go into hiding with the Orion. But where do you hide a big ship without being seen?

"We'll try in the Persoons harbor in Rotterdam," father suggested. "It is a long, narrow harbor with the backs of small industrial buildings on both sides. You are not as visible that way from the public road." So the Orion sailed empty from IJmuiden to Rotterdam. At the Steenplaat in Rotterdam a quantity of water was taken into the hold so the ship came to lay deeper and was less noticeable that way.

At dusk father sailed backwards into the harbor. The Orion was moored as inconspicuously as possible between the other ships that were there already. The mast and other parts that stuck out were taken down. Next father and Jan painted all the light colors of the ship with dark paint. And that way they hoped to wait for the end of the war without interference. Once every two weeks father went to get the mail from relatives in South Rotterdam. At the same time he then heard the latest news of the relatives. The war news he heard on board via the English transmitter.

After about five weeks a neatly dressed gentleman with a hat suddenly stepped on board the Orion. Mother was in the cockpit and saw him coming. Father was in the deck-house.

Mother called: "Father, come and have a look, somebody is coming on board." Father went upstairs.

"Look there," mother said and pointed to the man.

After a few moments father said: "You know who that is? That is your youngest brother."

"Yes," mother said, "now I see it too." She opened the door of the cockpit to let her brother enter. He stepped inside and they greeted each other.

"How are you?" mother asked.

Her brother laughed, "As you can see I am fine."

"Come to the deck-house," mother said, "then we'll have coffee. You like some?"

"Please," he said.

"How did you know we were here?" mother asked.

"I went to ask at your mailing address where I could find you," he said, "and they sent me here."

"How are father and mother?" mother asked.

"Oh, they'll be fine. I haven't been home for a long time."

"What kind of work do you do?" mother asked.

"Oh, some of this and that," he said. "I often go along with a cargo-train to Germany."

"Do the Germans make you do that?" she asked.

"No," he answered, "but I have to live and make some money."

"What is in that train?" she asked.

"Oh, a bit of everything," he answered.

"But what is it?" she insisted.

"Usually horses," he said.

When the coffee was gone the conversation halted and he said good-bye.

"Strange bird," father said. "Always was," mother said, "must be because he is the youngest."

Only after the war did it become clear why oom Fien had been so reserved. His travels to and from Germany, with a German identity card, served as a cover. In reality he worked for a resistance organization in Amsterdam. During one of his trips to Germany the group in Amsterdam was raided by the Gestapo. A brother-in-law of oom Fien was present too. Only oom Fien was left.

Confiscated

The next morning a German tugboat sailed into the Persoons harbor. A few German soldiers stood on deck and looked carefully around. They moored the tugboat alongside the Orion. Jan had seen them arriving and gave father a signal.

"Watch carefully," father said, "I won't show myself and will stay in the deck-house."

The captain of the tugboat stepped on board the Orion and asked Jan if his father was on board.

"Yes, sure," Jan said. He walked to the back of the ship to call his father. The captain followed on his heels and stepped into the deck-house right behind Jan.

Father had already heard them and came upstairs.

"Are you the skipper?" the captain asked.

"Yes," father said.

The captain handed father an envelope with papers.

"It says in here that your ship is seized by the German army. You will directly come along to the Waal harbor to load for Magdenburg." Jan could see father's alarm.

"To Magdenburg?" he stammered.

"Yes," the captain said, "prepare your ship for sailing and I will take you to the Waal harbor, you make sure you're ready tomorrow morning for loading. You will then receive more instructions. Make sure the water has been pumped out of the hold and that it is dry. During the time you are in Rotterdam you will have a soldier on board as guard. If you do as you are told you don't have to expect any problems."

"Things can turn out strange," father thought, "yesterday there was a man on board who transports horses to Germany and today my ship is confiscated."

Quickly father and Jan made the Orion ready for sailing. They had no desire to get Germans on board to do that. The tugboat went around meanwhile and attached a towrope. The mooring cables of the Orion were detached and neatly stowed. The mast was put up straight again and the flag hoisted.

"We are ready to sail," Jan called to the crew of the tugboat.

With quite a speed the Orion was towed out of the Persoons harbor then, taken to the Waal harbor and moored on pier 5.

Loading for Germany

Because father and Jan had worked all night, first to pump the water out of the hold and after that to dry out the hold, loading could be started early next morning. With a hoisting crane parcels were placed in the hold consisting of packages of rye-bread, wrapped airtight in cellophane. After loading for two days 250 tons of rye-bread were in the hold.

"Well," Jan said to father, "we have to make such a long trip with that? Before we get there it will be covered with mold. But at the front in Russia they aren't used to much."

Father asked the soldier on guard duty when the ship's papers would be ready and the Orion could leave.

"I haven't had any orders yet," the soldier said, "you wait and see."

The next day, some time in the morning, the German tugboat sailed into the Waal harbor and moored alongside the Orion. The captain stepped across and said to father, "You will stay here with your ship until the day after tomorrow. There is more to go to Germany."

"I don't get it," father said. "They can't put another load on top of the rye-bread. Well, we'll see."

That day a tanker came alongside and the fuel tanks of the Orion were filled up. The ship was cleaned and prepared for a big trip. Mother went on shore and used all the ration coupons, they would have expired before they returned anyway, if they returned. Father went to get the mail and inform the relatives about the big trip. When everyone was back on board again that evening mother said they should go to bed early and have a good nights sleep, because it might be the last one for a while.

Next morning when Jan went into the cockpit after coffee break he saw a tug sail into the Waal harbor. Behind the German navy tugboat two barges were attached, also called 'Amsterdammertjes.' They came in their direction and moored alongside the Orion.
"What's the good of that?" Jan thought. "There is plenty of room in front of and behind the Orion."
On the barges large pieces of a load were resting, covered with camouflaged tarps.
On both barges were two soldiers dressed in brown uniforms. After the barges were moored the captain of the tugboat came to father and said, "You have orders from the senior officer to take the two barges to Magdenburg. Beneath the tarps is a dismantled American bomber. They call that a 'flying fort.' The airplane made an emergency landing in the vicinity of Haarlem and came to us undamaged. It has to be taken to an airplane factory in Magdenburg for inspection. There will probably be apparatus in the airplane that we don't know about yet. The soldiers going along as guards have plenty of provisions for themselves, and also for your family."
"But," father said bewildered, "my ship can hardly get to Germany itself, how can that be done with those two barges behind?"
The captain had to laugh about what was, in his eyes, a stupid question.

"That's no problem," he said, "from here to Nijmegen you'll get a tugboat and from Nijmegen to Germany you'll get an even stronger tugboat. That tugboat will take you to the entrance of the Wesel-Dartteln canal. From there you can do it yourself. Also you will get papers that will give you right of way everywhere in order to get to Magdenburg as quickly as possible. Do you have any other questions?"

Father stood perplexed and stammered, "No, no,"

"Then I wish you a good trip. Tomorrow morning at six o'clock the tugboat will be here." With this announcement the captain left the Orion.

That evening there was a long conversation in the deckhouse of the Orion about the adventure that was waiting for them. But the core of the conversation was the question, "How did the Germans know that the Orion was hidden in Rotterdam?" There were some painful suspicions, but father and mother did not talk about it with the children.

"What about the children who are going to school?" mother wondered, "maybe we won't be back in Holland before the end of the war. Or they may send us to Russia with the rye-bread. Once you're sailing on the Elbe that's not that far away."

"I don't know either," father said, "let's trust that everything will work out OK."

"Then I better write the children a long letter," mother said.

On the way to Magdenburg

The next morning, even before six o'clock, Jan woke to the noise of a ship's propeller. He quickly jumped out of his bed and got dressed. Once upstairs he saw that a large tugboat had moored alongside the barges. Painted gray all over and with a number on both sides of the bow. On the quarter-deck of the tugboat he saw a winch. This showed him that it was a Rhine tugboat commandeered by the Germans.

"Wow," Jan thought, "that's a powerful tugboat, it must have an engine of 750 hp. What awesome power compared to the engine of the Orion which only has 75 hp."

The captain of the tugboat stood talking with father. By the looks and sound of him he seemed a nice man. Unnoticed Jan stood so close to them that he could hear the conversation.

"I have always sailed on the Rhine," the man said. "I was born and bred in Rudersheim. I have towed many Dutch ships up the Rhine. But, because of this dirty war your best friends become your enemies."

"What tugboat was this originally?" father asked, "I must have seen her before."

"You probably know her," the captain said, "she is the Frauenlob VI."

"Indeed," father said, "that was one of the most beautiful tugboats of the Middle-Rhine."

"Well let's go," the tugboat captain said, "we still have a long trip ahead of us. We sail from six o'clock in the morning till eight o'clock at night. I expect to be at the Wesel-Dartteln canal in less than three whole days."

"But," father said, "I thought we would get a different, more powerful tugboat in Nijmegen?"

"No, no," the captain said, "that was changed. Originally I would take you from Nijmegen to the Wesel-Dartteln canal, but since I was in Rotterdam anyway I was ordered to take you along."

"How strong is the engine in your tugboat?" father asked.

"One thousand hp," he answered.

"Good grief," Jan thought, "one thousand hp, that is something else. Now we will sail fast."

"If necessary on the way, for example during an air raid, we will sail between the piers for protection. Nobody may leave the ship and go on shore without my permission. If there are pressing reasons for talking to me during the trip, hoist and lower the flag several times. As you see, in front of the cockpit of the tugboat is a machine-gun nest. If we are attacked, we will defend ourselves with it. Do you have any other questions? If not, then I hope we'll have a good trip. I will give you a towrope of 22 mm in diameter and with it tow you at a length of about one hundred meters. I know from experience that your ship is difficult to steer and I can intercept the sheer myself that way."

Then he stepped on board the tugboat.

Meanwhile the crew of the tugboat had put the barges behind the Orion and attached them with heavy steel cables.

"Well, well," Jan thought, "it looks like they're never supposed to come off again."

When everything was in order the tugboat sailed to the front of the Orion and father was given a heavy steel cable, the so-called 'strang.' Jan helped him to lay the unwilling strang with at least five crosswise loops around the two bollards and tie them together with rope. When this was ready father went back to take the helm.

"Throw the mooring cables on shore loose now, Jan," he called.

Meanwhile the tugboat slowly sailed ahead until the strang became tight and was lifted out of the water, it crunched around the bollards.

"Everything loose," Jan called.

"Good," father said, "hoist the tow flag to the top of the mast, then we'll leave." Jan heard that the engine of the tugboat turned over faster and that the propeller water was pushed back with force.

"What a beautiful sound a four-stroke engine makes," he thought.

The Orion made good speed and soon after, they sailed out of the Waal harbor, up the Nieuwe Maas, in the direction of Germany.

"We're already going fast," Jan said to father, "look at that bow wave we make."

"Oh," father said, "he is still taking it easy next to the city. You'll see, once we are past the anchorage of Merode then he will push on."

And sure enough, when they passed the anchorage after one hour of sailing Jan heard, standing next to the cockpit of the Orion, that the engine of the tugboat started to turn faster. The water boiled with more and more speed on both sides of the Orion, it was scary to see.

"If you get tired of steering," Jan said to his father, "I can take over for a while."

"Well, that's great," father said, "but it is heavy to steer with those barges behind as well, if necessary you can help." Meanwhile the younger children stood looking with their little noses glued to the windows of the cockpit. When, after some time, they came to Papendrecht and sailed up the river Noord in the direction of Beneden Merwede, a German patrol boat came towards the German tugboat with much showing of flags and high speed.

"Let's see now if we'll get right of way everywhere," father said.

The patrol boat sailed at a distance of about five meters beside the tugboat. Next to the cockpit a German soldier stood with a gun under his arm. The captain appeared in the doorway of the cockpit. He held a megaphone in his hand and called out something in the direction of the tugboat. The captain of the tugboat opened the door of the cockpit and held his hand up to his ear as if to say, "Excuse me?"

Meanwhile the tugboat did not stop, but continued at full power. After the tugboat captain had heard what the man on the patrol ship had to say he also grabbed the megaphone and called something back. The result was amazing. The soldier next to the cockpit jumped to attention. The captain of the patrol boat waved and called something to the helmsman. The patrol boat turned away sharply and sailed in the other direction.

"Well," father said, "the tugboat captain was right. They know who we are and what we are transporting."

After sailing for a day and a half the tug reached the Dutch-German border without any problems. Before the tugboat stopped to carry out the customs formalities a green customs boat came alongside. One man stepped over onto the tugboat and two men were dropped off on the Orion. They were friendly and in good humor. After looking at the papers and stamping the passports they stepped onto the two barges. In a moment they were done there and signaled the patrol boat to pick them up. While walking past the cockpit they wished father a good trip and good-bye. They stepped over onto the patrol boat and the trip was continued.

The same ritual was repeated an hour later at the German border in Emmerick. Except they used more rigmarole there. Clicking of heels and calling of 'Hail Hitler' was heard everywhere. Several German officials were curious about the warspoils and went to have a look on board the barges. Their amazement was great. They said that they had never seen such an enormous giant-airplane. "But they have heard it," Jan thought to himself with the trip to the Ruhr in mind. Without asking about anything they left the ship and departed.

The trip was continued and the next day, after noon, the Wesel was reached where the opening to the Wesel-Dartteln canal is. The Orion was moored in front of the lock. The tugboat wound her strang on the winch-drum and came alongside.

"There, we did that quickly and without problems," the captain said to father.

"Indeed," father said, "if the rest of the trip goes just as quickly we'll soon be rid of it."

The captain shook hands with father and mother and left. The tugboat was thrown loose and sailed away. First the fuel-tanks were filled up. Then father and Jan went on shore to buy bread. That was no problem. Bread, meat and milk were available in plenty. And they had already received rationing-cards in Rotterdam.

Back on board the Orion father finally had time to have a little talk with the soldiers on board the barges. They appeared to be friendly people. There were four of them and they sort of lived in the airplane. Their orders were that at all times one of them had to keep watch. They had to prevent sabotage. They invited father and mother to have a look in the airplane. Everything was strange for the soldiers too and they were not able to tell much about technical points. The children were allowed to come and look also. Jan stared his eyes out. Unbelievable, so many little clocks and meters in the cockpit.

Piles of bullets lay in the gun-turrets. Only the bomb racks were empty. That could be a sign that the plane had run into problems on the way back to England. Father asked if it was not dangerous to transport all that ammunition. Not usually according to the soldiers, but during an air raid it could become dangerous.

Father noticed that the men were glad to talk and invited them for a cup of coffee that evening. That did not fall on deaf ears. And so that evening two of the four men came for coffee. One was trying to contact his wife in Giessen. The fourth thought he should dutifully stay with the plane. Later it turned out that he was a real fan of Hitler. One of them brought a piece of plastic from a broken gun-turret along that evening. Much later father made a little ring with this for one of the girls.

Once, after a long day's sail when the Orion was moored with her tug, two of the German soldiers went swimming. For convenience sake they went in their birthday-suits. The little ones were already in bed. Only Ina and Jan were still up. When mother saw what was going to happen Ina was sent to the deck-house.

"Go downstairs to read or something," mother said.

Ina did go to the deck-house, but instead of reading she climbed on the couch and peeked at those strange fellows through the port-hole.

During the long days sailing the three soldiers took turns to come to the cockpit of the Orion for a chat. And that is how a relationship of trust started. The fourth one hardly ever came out of the airplane, he probably felt responsible for the other soldiers and the spoils of war.

One of the men told father that he had a small farm in Beieren. Four cows provided for a modest income for the family, made up of father, mother, a twenty year old son, who was a soldier in Russia and a fifteen year old daughter. With two horses he worked the land. For a long time he was able to stay out of the paws of the Wehrmacht, but informants did not sleep in Germany either. He had to report at the city-hall and was conscripted for surveillance duty because of his age. He was lucky to be stationed in Holland. "For the same token they send you to Russia or Poland," he said. His wife and daughter did the farm work together. He hoped for a speedy end to Nazism.

"Maybe I'll see my son back yet," he said and had to blow his nose all of a sudden. "But don't say that to the man who is standing guard just now, he thinks differently about it than I."

The second soldier was the owner of a small print shop in a small town under the smoke of Hannover. Both his co-workers had been called up for military duty earlier. He himself kept working as long as he could, together with his wife. But because of a shortage of manpower in the army he was taken from his bed and put on surveillance duty. He was worried about his wife. They had no children.

"And all that for a crazy corporal," he sighed.

The third soldier gladly came to chat but he guarded his tongue. Either he was scared of number four or he was ashamed of the decline of Germany.

It was a long trip through the beautiful Wesel-Dartteln and Dortmund-Eems canal. For days on end they sailed through a glorious landscape where forests stretched on either side of the canal as far as the horizon and where once in a while even wild animals showed themselves. Sometimes a herd of deer, then again a few wild boars.

Near the town of Rheine the Orion turned into the Mittelland canal. Several times that day there were delays. When they approached industrial areas such as, for example, near Osnabruck, they could not sail because of artificially created fog. The fog was to prevent the Allied planes from seeing the targets they wanted to bomb.

Once in a while during the trip they would moor in a small village. Some of the soldiers would go on shore then to get supplies. Heavily laden they would get back and give mother part of it, among other things the famous German sausage.

But a nasty conflict happened on the way. While father was at the helm he saw, a few kilometers in front of the ship, a big American bomber flying at low height. It flew over the canal at an angle and left a black trail of smoke that came from one of the engines.

Father called to mother, "You see that? That plane is on fire and is going to crash."

"Oh dear," mother said, "those poor fellows."

When it got a little closer they saw small black dots coming from the plane. Soon after six parachutes appeared. At the same time mother heard shooting from the barge. When she looked around she saw that the soldier they had been warned about was shooting at the parachutists with a carbine. She jumped out of the cockpit and started calling to the soldier with clenched fists. Father quickly went after her and pulled her back into the cockpit.

"Stay here and keep your mouth shut," he said.

"That wretch," mother said, "that rotten Hun. Shoot at defenseless people, that's what they're good at."

"You're totally right," father said, "but we are sailing in enemy territory with children on board. If he wants to he could imprison you." Sulking, mother disappeared into the deck-house.

"Look at that, father," Jan said, "one of the parachutes is swinging badly back and forth. He must have been hit and can't steer his parachute anymore." A sad event that fortunately brought no consequences for mother's hotheaded behavior.

In Hannover they moored. The guards had to make contact with a certain army detail. They came back with the announcement that because of the low water level in the river Elbe the Orion could sail no further than Haldensleben and would be unloaded there. The barges, which had much less draught than the Orion, could go on to Magdenburg with a special tugboat. The next day the Orion sailed on and delivered the barges down from the lock in Wolmirst that gives access to the Elbe. After waiting for a few days the order came to sail back to Braunschweig to unload the rye-bread there instead of in Haldensleben.

During the unloading terribly bad weather broke loose. A lightening flash hit the fore-mast. The wood was burned black.

Fortunately the airplane with the ammunition had been delivered already. When the Orion was unloaded father got written permission to sail the empty ship to Dortmund. This was a relief for everyone. At least that was in the direction of Holland. The trip back with the empty ship took just as long as the trip there with the loaded ship. The Orion had after all no more priority status and had to wait for her turn. After four or five long days sailing the Orion was moored in Dortmund. Father reported to the senior officer and was informed that the Orion had to load in the Rhein harbour for Hengelo in Overijssel. In the spring of 1944 the Orion arrived in Hengelo. The trip had been full of suspense but ended well.

The End Approaches

The end of the war kept coming closer. Below the big rivers Holland had already been liberated. During a clear night you could see the fire of the anti-aircraft guns light up the sky surrounding Arnhem. At night too it was noticeable by the thousands of Allied planes that flew over to do their destructive work in Germany.

The Orion was unloaded in Hengelo and father got the order to sail to Lochem with the empty ship. There he had to report again. Already the day after leaving Hengelo they moored in Lochem. While father was on shore the rest of the family sat in the cockpit. All of a sudden a rowboat with three German soldiers appeared next to the ship. They waved in a friendly manner and started to fish. No, not with a rod but with explosives. One of them held a hand-grenade in his hand. Obviously a projectile because of its long handle. The soldier stood in the middle of the rowboat, pulled the safety-pin out of the grenade and wanted to throw it into the water. But before he had a chance the rowboat moved because the two other soldiers shifted their position. He lost his balance, threatened to fall and let the hand-grenade drop into the rowboat. In the blink of an eye all three jumped overboard.

The explosion that followed severely damaged the rowboat and it filled with water. Soon after, a few fish floated to the surface. The three soldiers got off all right. They swam to shore and climbed out of the water. Soaking wet they went back to their quarters.

Father reported to the receptionist of the senior officer in Lochem and was shown a place where he could wait till he could go to see the senior officer. He was kindly received, but was told that the Orion would be confiscated for the second time and had to sail for the Germans again. A soldier would be placed on board as guard. They were free to go where they wanted, except father was not allowed off the ship.
Father protested vehemently and suggested that he would surrender the ship and then live on shore with his family. However the senior officer would not have anything to do with that.
"We have no other people to sail the ship," he said. "You stay on board and your wife and children may come and go as they wish. You load here in Lochem: logs for Zwolle."
Then father could leave. When he got back on board a soldier in a brown uniform stood on the bow with a gun over his shoulder. In two days time 300 tons of logs were loaded in Lochem. Beautiful beach logs, destined for the furniture industry.
The next night there was a full moon and you could read the newspaper outside. So it was perfect flying weather. That night English fighter planes flew along the Twente canal and shot at anything that looked like a ship. When they came close to the Orion, which could not be seen from the air because of overhanging tree limbs, the guard thought he had to shoot at the fighter planes with his gun.

When father talked to him about it the next day and pointed out the stupidity of it, he got an ear full. Father then discovered that the soldier was of Belgian descent and enlisted in the German army because he thought the Nazis would improve the world. Also that day it turned out that the English fighter planes had a successful night behind them. Their order probably was: "Damage the lock works in the Twente canal, but don't destroy them." At least that is what the Orion experienced in Eefde.

That is where the lock is that, counting from the Gelderse IJssel, is supposed to keep the watermark at the right level in the Twente canal. During a low water level in the Ijssel, and that was the case at that time, there is a difference of eight to nine meters. On both sides of the lock there are vertical lift-doors. These are moved up and down with powerful electric motors. While open, the doors are cranked up into high lifting-towers so the ships can sail underneath. In the middle of the lock-complex is a control-building, from which the electric motors are worked.

That night the lifting-towers and their winches were not attacked by the airplanes and damaged, but only the control-building. This was put out of order. With the result that the shipping traffic was not totally stopped, but ran into serious delays. From then on the doors could only be cranked open and closed by hand.

The next day the Orion sailed from Lochem to Eefde and moored in front of the lock. There were four other ships waiting to leave the canal and three to go in through the lock. Father went to the lock to see if there was a possibility of going through the lock that day. But that was disappointing. The lock-master let him know that if he wanted to go through the lock he had to come and help on the lifting-tower as soon as it got dark. Then one half would be turned open by hand and later the other let down. All high parts on the ships had to be removed in order to be able to go under the doors as soon as possible.

A minimum of six people was needed to turn for four hours, first in one lifting-tower and then in the other. Jan had stayed on board with Ina and mother and the young ones. Apparently the soldier in the bow was bored and asked if mother would like a drumstick. Jan thought she would, why not? At that the soldier took his gun and shot at a chicken in the farmyard of a farm about one hundred and fifty meters away. Fortunately the soldier missed. The chickens scattered in every direction. He must have been close with his shot.

Next the soldier took a hand grenade, pulled the pin and threw it into the canal. Soon after a heavy explosion followed and a fountain of water sprayed up, that took along a large amount of fish. Because of the explosion they were dead immediately. Jan fished a meal out of the canal and took it to mother. The other children were playing on shore, they were frightened by the bang and ran like hares back on board, where they were caught by mother.

A Hard Night

In the evening, when it got dark and there would probably be no airplanes because of the clouds, father went to the lock. First he did not want Jan to come along, but after lots of nagging he was allowed after all. Together they climbed up the metal stairs in the lifting-tower.

There they met more skippers. In the lifting-tower were enormously big winches around which the ropes turned that pulled up the door. At both ends of the winches handles had been attached on the cog-wheels. In the large wheel there were about one hundred and fifty and in the small wheel about twenty cogs, this made for a significant reduction. With six people the handles were put in motion. After four hours of uninterrupted turning the door had been lifted enough so ships could sail underneath. Quickly the ships sailed into the locks and the turning-game could start again, but this time to let the door down. By seven o'clock the next morning the door was down again. But the ships were now in a trap, because they could not leave at the other end.

Thankfully, because of the bad weather that day, they could continue turning without interference from airplanes and by the afternoon they had the door ready for the ships to sail out of the lock. As soon as they could find a spot the Orion was moored.

"Aren't we sailing further?" Jan asked.

"Not today," father said, "and I don't think you'll be sailing along tomorrow. I talked to the lock-master last night and asked if he happened to know an address where mother can stay with you all while I continue on to Zwolle. Later I will go with mother and take a look where it is and then I will take you all there late this evening."

The Move

In order not to have any trouble with the fanatical soldier father had to discuss it with him. When father told him about his plans to leave mother and the children behind and to look for shelter for them the soldier agreed, if he could come along with father. He could not do anything else but agree. So father, mother and the soldier went on their way to the stated address. Farmer Ebbink had no objections. Mother was allowed to set up house on the threshing-floor in the daytime and sleep in the attic of the pig barn at night. There was lots of straw. According to the farmer they were not the first skipper's family to find temporary shelter there. Cooking was allowed only in the cookhouse because of the danger of fire. But they should shortly look for other shelter.

Quickly blankets and clothes were picked up on board and taken to the farm. Some provisions were also taken along. Father ordered Jan to quickly draw two cans with twenty liters of fuel from the fuel tanks and to take these, without the soldier noticing, to the farm. Later this idea turned out to be worth gold. Fuel was a desirable object of trade to the farmers.

When the children lay on their straw in the attic, where the oldest had to take care of the youngest, father came to say goodbye. With a fearful heart mother let him go.

"Will you be careful?" she asked. "Come back as soon as possible and let that soldier stew in his own juice."

"I'll try to leave as soon as possible," father said, "but now is not a good time, because he knows where I would be going. Then it is no sweat to find me. He can't be trusted. See you all later." Father went alone with the soldier back to the Orion, many thoughts went through his head: "What will the future bring?"

Mother, Ina and Jan cleaned the threshing-floor and then also went to the attic of the pig barn. The little ones were already asleep. The older children were still awake. They heard mother stumble up to the attic.

"Are you asleep yet?" she asked.

"No, I can't sleep," she heard one of the children say, "everything tickles here."

"That's because of the straw," mother said. She looked for a place between the children so she would be close by if they should wake.

There was no light so everything had to be done by feeling. However, she could not sleep. Her thoughts were with father who would be traveling alone with that untrustworthy soldier. She hoped everything would end well. She also thought about the children at school. Since they had been sent to Germany with that airplane she had not heard anything from them. Would Zeeland be liberated yet? How did her father and mother manage at their advanced age? If only she knew something. Heh, what a nuisance, now she got itchy and ticklish too. That dirty straw! By morning she fell asleep. But only for a short while. The children were noisy very early. The itching started again. The little ones pressed close to her.

"Let's go outside," she said to Ina and Jan, "careful on the stairs."

When they were all downstairs they went in a row to the warm threshing-floor. The cows looked up oddly when they came in. Milking was just finished.

"Give me a jug," the farmer said to mother, "then I'll put some milk in it for you."

"That's very kind," mother said, "I'll pay later."

While mother made a sandwich for everyone she realized that all the children were scratching their heads. At the same time she noticed that she was very itchy too. She called one of the children to her and went outside with it. In bright daylight she could see better. When she pulled the hairs apart she got a bad start. The scalp was gray with lice. They swarmed everywhere.

With leaden feet she went to the farmer's wife to tell her, but she only laughed about it. She said that before them another family had slept in the pig barn attic and she had seen that they were not so prim. That must be why. She would ask her husband to look for another place for the coming evening. This could not go on. "Yes, well," mother thought, "in the meantime we are all covered, how will we get rid of them?" Fortunately she had taken a fine-tooth comb along. Everybody was combed furiously, and then she gave herself a turn. Then the heads were dabbed with a cotton ball with alcohol. It hurt for a second, but was better than that irritating itch.

Escape

Early in the morning the Orion departed Eefde for Zwolle. They left the entrance canal to the lock and sailed with the current. That went nice and fast. Without any problems they sailed past Deventer and got to Zwolle in good time. During the trip the soldier showed a very different side. He made sure that father got bread and coffee. He told him that he had had a difficult youth in the mining area of Belgium—poverty reigned, father drinking, mother always sick. And he had to take care of his little brothers and sisters.

When he was twenty years old he was sick and tired of that. He went to an employment office and there they told him he could get a much better life if he conscripted in the German army. That is what he did. For three years he lived without any worries. But now it looked like that too would end. He had also heard that the German Reich was on the verge of collapse and then what? The last bullet in his gun he would save for himself. But before the Orion got to Zwolle father had talked him out of that. A little later he begged for an old civilian suit of father's. He wanted to try to go back to Belgium. "We'll see," father said, "you bet on the wrong horse, so don't expect a prize."

In Zwolle the Orion unloaded the wood and sailed empty to Meppel at the command of the Germans. They moored in front of the warehouse of the local gin-distillery. The next day under heavy supervision of the Germans a start was made to load four hundred wooden barrels of practically pure gin.

"Where does this load have to go?" father asked the German guard captain.

"The load is going to Germany before the Americans get here," he said.

"How do I get there?" father asked, "via the Rhine or via the Eems canal?"

No, via the Rhine could not be done anymore. The Americans were already in Arnhem. They must hurry to get away via the north. Father was seized with alarm. "To Germany? Further away from his family?" Sadly he sat in the deck-house thinking about what he could do. Suddenly he knew. When the loading was finished the soldiers would leave and only the guard would stay. Father did not have to be scared of him. He would leave his ship the Orion behind for the Germans and go back to his wife and children.

When all the barrels were stowed in the hold a German official came to bring a handful of papers.

"Early tomorrow morning you have to leave and sail on as fast as possible," he said to father. He left and took all the soldiers along. Father was left alone with the guard.

The soldier went in the bow to make his meal and wanted to go to sleep early. "That works out well," father thought. He changed his clothes and quietly left the ship. The soldier did not notice anything. Before turning the corner father looked once more behind him at his ship. He swallowed a few times and stepped out briskly to the train station. He was fortunate. A few minutes after buying a ticket to Zutphen the train pulled into the station. Father looked around for the soldier but no, fortunately he was nowhere to be seen.

"Well," father thought, "tomorrow morning is better, then I'll be a long way away."

In Zwolle he was not so fortunate. There was no other train to Zutphen that night, that was too bad. He decided to stay overnight at the station in the waiting room in order to continue on with the first train. The wooden benches were not very comfortable and so he woke up early. He ate a sandwich he had brought along. Coffee was not to be had so he took a few sips of water to flush down the bread. At six o'clock the train to Deventer left. It was still quiet in the train, but when they entered Deventer it teemed with German soldiers.

"What are they doing here?" father thought, "I don't trust this. Better not go on to Zutphen, better get out and go."

Quickly he stepped off the train and walked along unnoticed with the stream of passengers who were going to work in Deventer. He went to the bicycle-racks and hung around there until he heard the train leaving. He asked the owner of the bicycle-racks if he had an old bike for sale.

"Yes sir," the man said, "for fifteen guilders I have a pretty bike for you. But I can't answer for the quality of the tires; they are not so good anymore. What do you expect after four years of war?"

Father paid and left. At a steady speed he rode in the direction of Gorssel. From there it was only five kilometers. After biking for about half an hour he came to Eefde and after some searching found the farm where he had left his family. It was a happy reunion. A large portion of fear disappeared, they were together again. But in the background was the question of what the Germans would do when they heard father had escaped.

The soldier on board knew exactly where father had left his family. If he wanted to he could betray everything. What would happen to the Orion? The ship father had had built himself and where a lot of joys and sorrows had been shared? Mother told him the lice story. He could laugh about it. When they all lay down on clean straw in a different place that evening mother also thought the lice plague far behind her.

That night the roaring cannons were clearly heard. But the family did not know yet of the lost battle for Arnhem. The liberation of Eefde would take longer than they expected.

Looking for a Place to Live

That day father went on his bike to several farmers to find better living accommodations. With the third farmer he was successful. After telling his story and asking for shelter the farmer was so kind as to offer him a small stone house to live in and an unused chicken shed to sleep in.

"If we can use that I'll be very thankful," father said.

"Oh, no need for that," farmer Berenpas answered, "in these difficult times we must help each other as much as possible. There is a small wagon to hook behind your bike. Take that along and bring your family and things here right away. I'll tell the hired hand to meanwhile empty the little house."

A few hours later the whole family and the scanty household articles were relocated to farmer Berenpas'. They had thanked farmer Ebbink for his help. While the children played outside, father, mother Ina and Jan made a start with cleaning the little house.

First the cobwebs were removed. Then the floor was swept and after that scrubbed with a bucket of soapsuds. Meanwhile farmer Berenpas had taken a table and four chairs from the attic and put them ready.

"I also have a wooden bench with a cushion," he said, "if you put that against the wall the children can sit on that." In the attic he found an old high-chair for Jaap. From the back of the barn he produced a stove.

"Shows again how some things may come in handy for a person," he said. "In the wood-shed is sawn wood. Use as much as you need, it all has to be split but Jan can do that."

The farmer's wife came to have a look as well. After introductions were made she looked around the little house. "It already looks like something," she said, "but how are you going to cook?"

"I don't know," mother said, "we have nothing, maybe we can buy something in the village?"

"Don't count on that," the farmer's wife said, "of the little that is left in the stores nothing is sold to strangers. But I'll go and have a look." A little later she came back with a pile of household stuff like pots and pans, plates and cups. She also brought some butter, cheese and eggs along.

"Tonight you can come and get some milk and the potatoes are in the barn, you can take as many as you want."

Father and mother thanked the farmer and his wife for their kindness. But now sleeping accommodations had to be made in order first. A door in the back wall of the little house was the entrance to the old chicken shed. Now it served as storage space for farm equipment. While father and Jan were busy bringing order in the chicken shed mother stuck her head around the corner and called, "Dinner." Father looked at Jan. Dinner, of what? There was nothing left. He was going to go to the village that afternoon to get bread.

When they went into the little house the children were sitting on the bench behind the table with beaming faces. On the table was a steaming hotchpotch: potatoes with turnips and bacon.

"How did you manage to get that ready so quickly?" father asked mother.

"The farmer's wife delivered that," she said, "those people are good to us."

It tasted delicious. After dinner father and Jan continued with renewed energy to clean the chicken shed. Leftover chicken manure and straw were removed and taken to the manure pile. The holes in the floor were covered with pieces of cardboard. Farmer Berenpas had an iron bedstead with a mattress that was not used anymore which father and mother could sleep on and father hammered together two plank beds for the children. A thick layer of straw was put in it, an old rug on top of that and blankets on top of that. Sheets were only available for father and mother. Mother could not do without because of the tickling on her chin by the blankets.

After dinner farmer Berenpas came for a minute to see how things were going. If there was anything else needed we had to let him know.

To father he said, "If the Huns come at night you can get to the Elzewoods via the chicken shed and over the barbed wire fence. There you can hide till they're gone."

"That's what I'll do," father said.

To mother he said, "Us farmers are used to eating a plate of porridge at eight o'clock in the evening. Oatmeal or rye meal. I'll come and get the little boy every evening to eat along. If I am not around send one of the other children to bring him over. For all the children there is not enough. You see, we have another family in the hall and we regularly get people in hiding on the way through. Try to sleep even though everything is strange."

"Good-night," father said, "you are very good to us."

Farmer Berenpas went away and father fastened the hook on the inside of the door. You never knew who or what would be prowling around. Later on there were sometimes fights about who would bring little Jaap for the porridge. Because usually the taker would also get a plate of delicious rye meal porridge.

"Come on, children," mother said, "it's time for bed, Ina and Jan, you too. It has been a busy day and the little ones don't like to be alone."

Father lit the kerosene lamp, called a 'vleermuis' (bat) and went ahead of the children to the sleeping quarters. When he stepped inside he saw in the light of the lamp two little eyes light up on the floor. However he did not pay any attention to it. The beds were round with straw. The bigger children even jumped on them while father put the little ones on top. It bounced beautifully. After tucking them in father turned the light in the lamp down and hung it on a rusty nail.

"There," father said to mother, "they are able to sleep."

After an hour father and mother went to bed as well. Exhausted they fell asleep. In the middle of the night mother woke up. She heard a racket and thought somebody was breaking in. Soon after she felt something move on the blankets and thought, "There you go, they're inside already." She gave father a good poke and whispered, " Wake up, there are robbers, they want to steal the blankets."

"What?" father muttered, "what's the matter?" He turned up the lamp so that the light fell on the blankets. He got a scare of what he saw. At the end of the bed sat two rats. Their eyes flickered in the lamplight. "I've already seen that once before tonight," father thought. He whistled between his teeth and they were gone.

"What was that all about?" asked mother, who stayed deep under the covers.

"Oh," father said, "two rats who think we are living in their house."

"What?" mother screamed, "rats in bed? Take the kids out, maybe they'll eat their toes."

Father had to laugh. "Of course not," he said, "we'll leave the light turned up then they won't come back." Mother did not trust it and took little Jaap in bed with her to be sure. The next day father and Jan plugged the holes in the floor good and tight, so the rats could not get through.

After breakfast father said to Jan, "Why don't you go to the farmer, there is not enough work here for both of us, maybe you can help the farmer."

"Oh, sure," the farmer said, "lots of work. Ask my son Gerrit-Jan what you can do." And so Jan became a farmhand.

In the meantime the summer of 1944 approached.

At a distance of about three hundred meters from the temporary quarters of the Deurwaarder family, at the edge of the Elzewoods, stood a farm belonging to the castle 'Het Elze.' The farm was occupied by the Gotink family, very nice people, who had contacted the Deurwaarder family. They, in turn, appreciated that very much. Back and forth visits were made and so father and mother with the children were invited to spend Christmas afternoon with them. There was even chocolate milk.

While the whole group stood singing well known Christmas carols around the organ there was a knock on the door. Farmer Gotink opened the door and saw a young German soldier who asked if he could come inside to sing along. The farmer did not refuse him and he brought him into the living room. During the singing the soldier was overcome with homesickness and memories of his parental home made the tears run down his cheeks.

Because of the early dusk and the dark lane with trees that they had to cross the Deurwaarder family went home early. Everyone was frightened when halfway down the lane they suddenly heard a German soldier, who was spouting drunken talk. When he noticed the family he came to them and declared in hardly discernible gibberish: "Germany Over All," and also that he had saved the last hand-grenade for himself. He turned a half circle and showed that he had five or six hand grenades on his belt. The last one he did indeed save for himself. A few months later, when the Elzewoods was liberated and Jan went once more through the lane, there lay the particular soldier. His skull, still in the helmet, lay some distance away from the rest of the body. What contradictions—that peace on earth would look so horrible.

Life of a Peaceful Countryman

Even life on a farm has its highs and lows. One of the lows was reached that week—a historic event. Farmer Berenpas had a loyal dog, a Saint Bernard. Where the farmer went, the dog went also. The family that lived under the same roof in their own apartment, had a Pekinese, a very small animal. As usual farmer Berenpas came for our little brother one evening for his porridge. The Saint Bernard followed in the farmer's footsteps. Suddenly the little Pekinese came around the corner of the house and ran loudly barking to the farmer, who was carrying Jaap. The Saint Bernard, probably jealous of little Jaap who got more attention from the farmer than she, growled deep in her throat, snapped at the little dog and bit the head off in one go. The little head hung loose by the skin of the neck. He'd made short work of it. Later farmer Berenpas said to mother to be careful with little Jaap and not leave him in the farmyard by himself if the dog was there too. We had seen what jealousy could lead to.

Jan showed himself to be a great help on the farm. He learned to milk, feed the pigs and work with the horses.

Farmer Berenpas was pleased with him and said one day, "Listen, Jan. It is getting dangerous for our Gerrit-Jan to show himself on the public roads. If the Germans see him they may pick him up. That's why tomorrow you will go to Wichem with the horse and gig, to the miller. You will take three bags of oats and bring them back as rolled oats. Start out early, because it is a long way there and back. I'll give you money and a drawing of the road you have to follow. The best way is to take side roads as much as possible. That way you have less chance of inspection. Make sure the horse doesn't get over tired."

The next morning Jan woke early. He was a little nervous. Making such a long trip all by himself, that was no trifle. At seven o'clock he left. He followed exactly the route as marked on the drawing and arrived at the miller's at ten o'clock. Several times he had seen German soldiers on the way, but because he was kind of small Jan had not attracted any attention.

"Where are you from?" the miller asked.

"I am from farmer Berenpas in Eefde," Jan said.

"Then you must have left early?"

"Yes, at seven o'clock."

"Stable the horse over there then and give it some feed. While I roll the oats, you can drink coffee and eat a sandwich with my wife in the house."

At one o'clock the miller came to the house and announced that the oats were done. He helped Jan harness the horse and lifted the bags of oats into the gig. He covered them well, so you could not see what they were. "Don't show anyone on the way what you have, because there are people who would commit murder for that," he warned Jan.

Jan paid the miller with the money he had been given and thanked him for his good care.

"No problem," the miller said, "you be careful and make sure you get home safely. Stay away from the Huns and greetings to the farmer."

At six o'clock that evening Jan was safely home again with the rolled oats.

"There, that will last us for a while," the farmer said, "you better go home now, it has been a big day. Here, take a bag of oats for your mother." Beaming, Jan thanked the farmer. Now he could really surprise mother. A little later the whole family feasted on the best oatmeal porridge you could imagine.

Making Molasses

That father would also be put to work by the farmer became obvious when the molasses jar was empty.

"We have to make molasses and that's a good job for you," farmer Berenpas told father. "When the beets come out of the pit, you clean them well with water. You cut them into little pieces and throw them into the cooking pot and add a little water. Then you bring them to a boil and leave them simmering until all the water has evaporated. What is left is molasses."

Father did not understand at all. A sugar beet makes sugar and not molasses!

But he did what the farmer asked him. It was a big job before all the beets were in the cooking pot in little pieces. But finally he could start cooking and dragged the necessary firewood to the cookshed. He made a fire under the 'beet soup' and brought it to a boil. A cover on the pot was not allowed, so it could be stirred regularly and the water could evaporate quickly. Slowly the contents of the pot got less. It was starting to get dark when father could feel the porridge in the pot getting thicker. An hour later the farmer thought the result good enough and said to just leave it standing until the next morning and put it in jars then.

The farmer and father walked away, but left the stirring-spoon in the pot. Jan did not think that was right. He took it out, let it cool off and started licking it. Well, that was good molasses. It tasted even better than the molasses you got at the store. The next day, when everything was in jars, father was given along a large jar of molasses. According to Berenpas, it tasted delicious in the rye meal porridge. He was right.

The Little White Church

On Sunday the Deurwaarder family walked the half hour to the little white church in the village of Eefde. Several people looked up when they saw the family enter. The second Sunday the minister was waiting for them.

"I have seen you in church several times, but I don't know you. I guess you don't live here?" he said to father. Father briefly told him the story of their journey and gave him the address where he could be found. The minister promised to come that same week and father welcomed him ahead of time.

A few days later the minister biked into the barnyard and dismounted in front of their 'country-house.'

"Come in and sit down, you must be tired after such a long bike ride," mother said.

Meanwhile father came in as well and the minister listened with attention to the experiences of the family. He was obviously sympathetic to the way the family had to live after leaving the ship in a hurry. But he also praised the farmer for the way in which he had received the family.

It appeared later that the minister had reported his visit at a consistory meeting. At that time he had also asked to collect some used children's clothing, so the family could stand the cold better. Shortly after, parcels with good used clothes were delivered and the minister gave father some money.

"When your account is only drawn from and nothing is added it is soon gone," he figured. And father thankfully accepted.

Years later father and mother met the minister once more in Veere. For the second time he witnessed a disaster, the big flood of 1953.

On Sundays the Deurwaarders walked for half an hour to the little white church in the village of Eefde.

The Betrayal

While working for the farmer Jan was also regularly invited for dinner. The farmer knew that food would be scarce for the large skipper's family in his farmyard. There would be delicious hotchpotch with meat on the farmer's table, but they always ate in the kitchen, even on Sunday. From the porch you could walk in and out of the kitchen. But the door from the kitchen to the hall and the fancy living room (parlor) was always locked. Jan never saw anyone go in or out of it. It was only later that he understood the reason for that.

For more than two years a Jewish couple lived in the attic of the farm 'De Voort.' Only the farmer, his wife and their children knew about it. Even the family that rented an apartment downstairs on the side of the farmhouse did not know. Looking back that was a good job, because several young ladies who lived with them had their heads shaved after liberation.[*]

In the attic at the front of the house farmer Berenpas and his son Hendrik Jan had build a cupboard-bed in such a way that it did not show on the outside that there was space that could be used as a hiding place. Only by climbing up with a stepladder and then lowering oneself through a hatch, was the space accessible. Usually son Herman also slept in the attic to help the

---

[*] This was a punishment for dating German soldiers.

people in hiding into their hiding place and take the stepladder away as soon as there was danger. Then he quickly crawled under the blankets of the Jewish people so it looked as if the bed was slept in only by him.

Hendrik Jan did not agree in principle with his parents on risking so much to hide Jewish people for such a long time. It was a necessity to help, but after a short period they should move on. Two years and longer was too much, he thought. For security reasons, at the start of the hiding time of the Jewish couple, farmer Berenpas had made an agreement with the patriotic village constable in Eefde, that he would give them a signal if there was any danger. The village constable would knock on the window then and shout: "You have to black-out better, I can see light!" This way the discovery of the Jewish couple had already been prevented several times. But the system was not infallible.

One day Hendrik Jan was busy in the barn taking care of the cows when two gentlemen stepped through the barn door and onto the threshing-floor. When they saw Hendrik Jan they said they were from the G.I.A. (General Inspection Agency). Hendrik Jan knew the gentlemen and asked what they had come for.

"We came to check if there are too many staples in the house such as potatoes, dried beans, butter and meat."

"You better go to father then," Hendrik Jan said, "because he is in the kitchen." And he pointed to the kitchen door. Now right next to the kitchen door stairs gave access to the attic.

When the men walked in the direction of the kitchen door Hendrik Jan saw that the first man went up the stairs to the attic. He got a big scare, after all he knew about the Jewish people in hiding. A sudden fury went to his head. He turned around and grabbed a four-pronged pitch fork that stood there and ran to the stairs.

He called, "Come back or I'll stab you on the fork and then you'll be a corpse."

The man who had not reached the stairs yet got scared when he saw Hendrik Jan, red with fury. With breaking voice he called something to his partner. When he came back and saw Hendrik Jan standing there with furious looks, he thought better of it and walked out of the barn. While walking past Hendrik Jan he said, "You'll hear more about this."

Again Hendrik Jan asked his father what they were doing. But he said, "We have to help these people to stay out of the hands of the Huns."

Some time later on a dark night, a group of Home Guards, fourteen in total, biked without lights in the direction of 'De Voort.' A few surrounded the farmhouse very quietly. The rest stood by the front door. One of them banged on the door and called: "Open the door or we will kick it in!"

Farmer Berenpas and his wife woke in alarm. The farmer quickly pulled on his trousers and opened the front door.

"Move," the Home Guards called, "we want to search the house."

The farmer stood in the middle of the door with his large frame and said, "Come back when it is daylight."

He realized the great danger the people in hiding were in. But that was not acceptable to the Home Guards. They aimed their rifles at the farmer and he moved aside. Meanwhile Hendrik Jan and Herman appeared in the hall. And even though both were the age to work for the Germans they were left alone. They were looking for something else after all. Herman turned around and ran upstairs to help the people in hiding into their hiding place. Afterwards he pulled the blankets smooth on the bed the Jewish couple had been sleeping in, so that it looked like nobody had slept in the bed. Next he went downstairs to join the others. They were all chased into the kitchen and there guarded by a Home Guard. Everybody shook with terror and suspense.

The Home Guards spread out through the house and inspected every room. In the attic one of them was so smart to put his hand under the blankets of the bed. And of course, the bed still felt warm and so had been slept in shortly before. There had to be people in the house. After that it was no great feat to forcefully break open all hollow spaces. This way the Jewish couple was soon found. With much show of power they were chased down the stairs. They were not allowed time to dress warmly. At the bottom of the stairs the farmer and his wife stood looking on in dismay.

While walking past, the Jewish woman said to the farmer's wife, "Pray for us."

In the kitchen the Jewish woman was able to grab a sharp butcher's knife and with it she cut both wrists. Blood was everywhere and mayhem reigned. Everyone dashed towards her to press the veins closed.

Meanwhile someone jumped on a bike and rode to Eefde to get the doctor. When, after a while, he arrived, he bound the wounds. One of the Home Guards who had been standing outside came into the kitchen and said to the doctor, "What a beautiful night."

"Yes," the doctor answered, "but also a terrible night."

He must have been thinking of the terrible fate that was waiting for the Jewish people.

Hendrik Jan was ordered by the Home Guards to put the horse to the carriage. The Jewish couple and farmer Berenpas were told to get in and Hendrik Jan was commanded to follow them to the train station in Zutphen. At the station they waited for daylight and next they went with the first train to Arnhem. At the House of Detention they were taken to a German official. Then the three of them were put against a wall and had to keep their hands above their heads.

"Now our last hours have arrived," farmer Berenpas thought. But that was not so.

After the carriage with the arrested people of De Voort left, the farmer's wife said to her children, "Father must be cold. He is not wearing enough clothes because he was taken from his bed."

It was decided to send Herman with a parcel of clothes for the farmer to the senior officer in Zutphen, to ask him to send the clothing to Arnhem. After a day and night in a cold room farmer Berenpas was sent home without any explanations. To everyone's relief he told them that the clothes had been given to him before nightfall.

The Jewish couple was transported to Germany. As far as is known they did not return alive to Holland. Much later it became known, that the daughter of an upright Dutchman was going out with a Home Guard and she had probably talked too much. The underground organization advised farmer Berenpas to flee to England, because he knew too much. But this he definitely refused. He did not want to desert his family and farm operation.

The Pipe Must Smoke

Berenpas had shown father twenty square meters of land to grow tobacco plants on. Pipe tobacco was not for sale anymore of course. The plants had grown very well and were ready for harvest. The leaves were tied in bundles and hung to dry in a dry, drafty place. When the tobacco leaves were dry enough they were packed in a box in bundles and send to a tobacco factory in Groningen. There the tobacco was fermented and spiced and after it was cut, neatly packaged in half pound packs. And by a miracle, after about six weeks father was notified that he could come and pick up the tobacco at the post office. Now he could smoke his pipe again.

He did not, however, get much pleasure out of it. Apparently, either the spice was no good, or the tobacco was bad, because after several months he got nicotine poisoning. He put the tobacco away and stopped smoking altogether.

That winter it froze very hard. At a distance of about a twenty minute walk along the train tracks was a beautiful little lake that was frozen solid. The ice glittered in the light of the full moon. At school several children had told Wim that it was good for skating.

"You come too, it's close by," they had said.

"I'd like to," Wim answered, "but I don't have any skates."

"That doesn't matter," one of the boys had said, "you can borrow a pair of mine."

"But I have a brother and sister who would also like to come," Wim remembered.

"Then I'll ask my uncle if he still has skates."

"Great," Wim said, "tonight I'll ask my father and mother if we are allowed to come." "With the three of us we'll be allowed sooner than by myself," he thought.

And sure enough, after lots of nagging they got permission to go along to the ice the next evening.

"Ina," mother said, "you're the oldest and you watch the boys."

They skated several nights to their heart's desire, but slowly the moon waned and it got too dark. And then the fun was over. Mother was happy about that. Every night she worried about her young folk. All for nothing of course according to the boys.

The Ammunition Train

The Allied war machine ran well and was not to be stopped. Further and further the armies pulled into Europe. Only in the neighborhood of Arnhem were there delays that ended in tragedy for thousands of soldiers. Also in the area of the farm the acts of war came closer. At a distance of three hundred meters from the farm stood a large country house called 'Het Elze.' A farm belonging to the house lay behind it. The garden and the forest formed an enormous triangle.

Alongside one side of the triangle ran the railway from Hengelo to Zutphen. A forest road formed the second side. It ran from Het Elze to the road with the farm of Berenpas on it. The third side was formed by a clay road running next to the farm and crossing the railroad. The inside of the triangle consisted for the most part of a forest with huge beach trees, with the lane to the country house running right through it.

Early one morning the Elzewoods and Het Elze teemed with German soldiers and their materials. They had been pushed back to behind the IJssel and had to dig themselves in again to stop the Allied armies. The troops around Zutphen were supplied by rail from Germany. Regularly an ammunition train passed on its way to Zutphen. So also on this beautiful day.

Behind every three rail cars the Germans had coupled a car with anti-aircraft guns. Next to the Elze woods the engineer saw that the signal was red. He braked the train and brought it to a stop. The Germans were not used to this. Nervously the guards walked to the front.

"What's wrong? Keep going, keep going. Next the Tommies will come. Is there sabotage?" they shouted. And sure enough, the words were hardly out of their mouths when they heard the howling sound of a diving English fighter.

Soon after the anti-aircraft guns crackled from the train. They could shoot all they liked but they did not hit the target—the fighters were better at it. Two flew lengthwise over the train one behind the other. With their weapons they opened the train up for long stretches. Then they pulled up and flew circles at a great height to watch the effect of their attack. They did not have to wait long. It looked as if the train burst. Exploding projectiles flew in all directions. There was smoke and fire for a long way around. In particular the exploding tank grenades posed a big danger for the surroundings. Only after about five hours did the explosions get less and there appeared to be an end to the supply. It was a brilliant stroke for the English fighters.

With their weapons they opened up the train for long stretches.

The V1 and the V2

Shortly after the destruction of the ammunition train Jan woke up in the middle of the night because of a low flying airplane. He jumped out of bed and looked out the window. And yes, there it came again. But he got a scare. Behind the airplane a big flame was visible. "It must be on fire," he thought to himself, "the plane will want to land somewhere or it will crash." He pushed father and whispered that a burning airplane was circling. Father flew out of bed, woke everybody and told them to get dressed quickly. He went outside with Jan to watch the regularly returning plane. After coming over three of four times they heard some distance away from the farm an enormous explosion. The plane had crashed.

"Poor fellows," said mother, who had come outside as well, "they also have a mother or wife and children. They do it for our freedom."

The next day everyone talked about the crashed plane. But the exact cause of the crash was not known by anyone. The next night the family had hardly settled down in bed when father heard the droning noise of a single airplane again. In his pajamas he went outside and saw a plane overhead with a big tail of fire at the back. The plane flew at great height and straight in a westerly direction. It had hardly gone past when a second one followed.

"Now what," thought father, "could this be the secret weapon Hitler was bragging about?"

Soon everyone knew that this was indeed the secret weapon that went by at a great height and belonged to the retaliation weapons aimed at England. That is why they were called V1. The V1's were fired off close to the German border. By the time they came over Eefde they already flew at a great height and in a straight course. It rarely happened that one crashed.

However, an even heavier weapon came along, the V2. That one was fired off much closer by, three kilometers at the most from the farm.

In the strictly guarded woods a number of trees were cut down and a runway was constructed for this guided weapon. Not a smooth runway of concrete, but one sloping up made of steel. From this runway the flying bombs were shot away. The runway was camouflaged with large green nets. Berenpas said that if you listened closely at night you could hear, in the direction of the Joppe farm, a lot of yelling people. Those were the prisoners who had to launch the bomb. Often something went wrong and prisoners perished. Shortly before launching they cried out in pangs of death and yelled out loud. A little later you heard the humming of the flying rocket. If that was lacking then something had gone wrong. After launching about one in five V2's left its course. It would start flying in circles and kept that up until the fuel was burned up, then it crashed. For the population this was like playing Russian roulette, who would be hit?

Now, fifty years later these flying bombs are still regularly found and detonated.

On a Bicycle Tour

When the work on the farm slowed down Jan had more free time and went to the village once in a while. There he met a skipper's boy his own age. He was called Lammy. He told Jan he lived in the village with his parents and sister. They had no acquaintances and lived a withdrawn life. Food was scarce and with much effort his mother managed to produce a simple meal every day.

Lammy asked Jan if he felt like going for a long bike ride once in a while. On the way they would knock on the doors of different farmers and ask for a sandwich. This was no sooner said than done. First they biked way into the back country, not many people would knock on a farmer's door there. The people where they knocked were always friendly. It rarely happened that they were sent away with empty hands. Some even gave a bag with rye or wheat along. Jan did not tell his parents what they were doing and let Lammy take home everything they were given. After all, with farmer Berenpas the family lacked nothing.

The Ammunition Depot

As mentioned before, the Elze woods teemed with German soldiers. One day a German soldier came into the farmyard and asked to speak to the farmer. Berenpas was told by the officer that they needed a barn to store ammunition. In alarm the farmer refused with the announcement that everything was in use. The German said that that did not make any difference and claimed a barn at the back of the barnyard. It had to be emptied. In a few hours the first trucks with ammunition would arrive. The farmer objected but the German did not give in. Father and Jan helped farmer Berenpas to empty the barn, while Gerrit-Jan was wise enough to stay in the background. They hardly had the barn empty when large trucks started driving into the barnyard. Everyone had to stay away when the trucks were unloaded and the load taken into the barn.

Mother's heart was heavy. She ordered the children to stay inside, because you never knew what they were up to. The next day the barn was filled with ammunition, from pistol bullets to tank grenades, landmines, and hand grenades. Berenpas was very worried, not only for his business, but more for all the people who had found shelter with him. He knew that one spark was enough to explode the whole barn and destroy everything for far and wide.

He called father and told him what he had in mind. On the other side of the road, against the edge of the woods, were three silage pits of which the last one was empty. That pit had a depth of two and a half meters and a diameter of four meters and one wall was made of reinforced concrete. He advised father to make a roof on the pit with Jan's help. Behind the haystack was plenty of wood, they could use some heavy lumber as rafters and throw rugs or rushes over the top and cover it up with a meter of soil. A little opening would serve as the entrance and exit.

In the daytime they could stay in the little house, but Berenpas preferred that at night all of them would sleep in the silage pit. The Germans were at the end of their rope and whatever they saw move at night they shot at. And so father and Jan fixed up the pit and renovated it into a bomb shelter. Only when the roof was on could the inside be finished. First a layer of straw was put down and blankets spread on top.

It was quite a procession as the family went off to bed that first night. The children were afraid to crawl into the bomb shelter without mother. When everyone had found a place father went outside for a breath of fresh air. After the children had slept for a while one of them woke up and had to use the bathroom.

"Father, we forgot the chamber pot," mother called.

"For Pete's sake. I'm not going back to the farm in the dark to get one. Just use that big pan we had soup in," father answered.

And so the little ones were allowed to sit on the big pan one by one. Father emptied the pan, crawled into the bomb shelter and put the steps to one side, so no unexpected company could come in.

The second night in the bomb shelter was very uneasy. Outside machine-gun fire could be heard. That was answered with gunshots. Canadian shock troops sent scouts to find out if any Germans were in the Elze woods. Well, there were plenty. The Canadians pulled back and it was quiet until morning.

Early that morning Berenpas came to the bomb shelter and called down for father to come up for a minute. Father put the steps in front of the exit and went outside.

"I think it's getting too dangerous for you here," the farmer said to father. "Suppose one of those crazy Germans throws a hand grenade into the bomb shelter, no one would come out alive. Wait until daylight, then walk straight through the fields to the farm of my brother. It is that farm," he pointed in the distance. "It is safer there than here. Tell him I sent you and ask if you can move into the basement."

Quickly father looked for a long stick and tied a white diaper onto it. When it got light outside the whole family walked in single file through the wet fields to the brother of Berenpas. Everyone carried something extra, while father carried the flag and the baby. Regularly they hid when they heard the cannons roar. After an hour's walk, the little ones only walked slowly, and after crawling under barbed wire fences, they came to the appointed farm. It was eerily quiet. No person or animal was to be seen in the farmyard. Father knocked on the door, but nobody opened it. He felt the doorknob and the door opened.

"Strange," he thought, "the door is unlocked and nobody home?"

He walked through a second and third door. This one opened up to the barn. On one side stood a row of ten or twelve milk cows. On the other side of the barn were a number of pens with pigs and calves. But even in the barn nobody was to be seen. Meanwhile mother and the children had come in too.

"You wait," father said, "and I'll see if anyone is home."

But no, there too nobody was to be seen even though everything was unlocked.

"Now there is still one possibility left," father said when he got back, "and that is that they are in the basement."

After looking around for a while he found the basement door, opened it and called: "Is anyone downstairs?"

"Yes, we're here," he heard someone answer. A little later the farmer appeared in the stair opening.

"We came from the farm of your brother in the Elze woods," father said. "It is getting too dangerous there and so your brother sent us here. He thought maybe we could sit in the basement with you?"

The farmer growled, "No, you can't. My wife and daughter are here as well and our food is in the basement. You can find a place in the barn."

In the barn father and mother arranged a place for the children as best as they could and ate the sandwiches they had brought along. When the children had played for a while the farmer and his daughter came to the barn to feed and milk. This gave a welcome diversion for the children. When he was done, the farmer left with his daughter to go to the basement again. Nothing had been said and no food or drink had been offered to the children. Father spread some straw on the floor for the children to sleep on. Then, finally, there seemed to be a moment of rest for father and mother. But that was only an illusion.

The roaring of the cannons that had started in the afternoon, continued without easing off and seemed to come closer all the time. At eight o'clock that night father went outside to have a look. When he came back in he softly said to mother and the two oldest children, "This will be a bad night. The shells are flying exactly over the barn we're in. I'll ask the farmer again if we can go into the basement as well."

He knocked on the basement door, but got no answer. After waiting a bit he opened the basement door and called: "Is anybody downstairs?" But nobody answered. "Strange," father thought, "where could they have gone to so suddenly?"

He went back to the barn and told mother what was going on.

"You know what?" father said, "I'm taking the oil lamp and I'm going to look in the basement. Maybe something happened and they need help. Jan, come along and stand at the top of the basement steps. If I need you I'll call."

"Yes, father," Jan said in a small voice. He thought it all pretty scary.

Father called once again and went down the basement stairs. He came to quite a large room, where alongside the walls shelves had been constructed that were loaded with canning jars and groceries. But there were no people.

"Could there possibly be a second basement?" father thought. But there was no door to be found anywhere. Father went upstairs again.

"Nothing to be found," he said to Jan.

"Then we should have a look in the bicycle shed," Jan said, "this afternoon there were bikes, if they are gone the people are gone too."

Father was hardly out the door when he saw the door of the bicycle shed open and not a single bike inside. When he went inside he said to mother, "You understand it? What a strange farmer. He won't say two words to us, but sneaks off and leaves the whole business and a barn full of animals to take care of itself."

"They must have been terribly scared," mother said.

"Come, we'll go into the basement, it's getting too dangerous here," father said. He carried a few of the children who were already asleep, downstairs. They were put down on the blankets left behind by the farmer and continued sleeping peacefully.

"You'd almost think the shells are coming closer all the time and just barely clear the roof," father said. "If only they won't cause a fire."

"Say, Jan, every basement should have an emergency exit, will you look for it and make sure the exit is clear? You never know, if there is a fire and we can't leave by the door, we'll have to use it."

Jan found the emergency exit in no time. There was a blacked out window in the basement that exited on the east side of the house. He put some crates on top of each other, so that in case of danger they could leave quickly. And the cannons continued to roar.

In the middle of the night mother jabbed father. She thought she could hear cattle lowing. Father got up and went out of the basement. When he opened the door to the barn he got a terrible scare. There was a strong smell of fire. And when he looked through a hatch to the loft he saw stars. Suddenly he could hear the roaring of a shell. Automatically he bend down and heard the shell go straight through the roof and continue on its way. The cattle got nervous and lowed piteously.

"Now what should I do?" father thought. "I never was very fond of cows, but if there is a fire they'll perish in a terrible way. How can a farmer get it into his head to leave?"

Quickly he went back to the basement and told what was happening.

"You stay here," he said, "I'll go back to the stable to cut the cattle loose."

He took the bread knife and left. In the basement it was deadly quiet. But with every shell flying through the roof everyone shrunk in fear because of father. Meanwhile he was in the dark stable. Everything was strange to him. He unfastened the latch of the door that opened onto the pasture.

Shaking with fear he stepped in between the two front cows. The animals lowed with fear and were deadly afraid. They both turned their head in the direction of father.

"Back off," he muttered, "then I'll cut the rope and you can go outside."

By sitting on his knees he could cut the rope of the first cow by reaching under the heads. As soon as the first cow noticed she was free she jumped back over the gutter and ran out the door to the outside. Father got a scare. When you yourself are low by the ground a cow's head looks even bigger than in reality. In this way he crawled from one cow to the next until they were all loose. He broke into a sweat. He was just going to stand with his back to the wall to rest when another shell flew through the roof.

"I have to get out of here," father thought, "the sooner the better."

But first the doors of the pig and calf pens had to be opened, so those animals could go outside as well. That did not take long. They ran for their lives.

"There," father thought, "now to the basement, it will be safer there than here."

But while he walked across the farmyard he heard a horse neighing in a closed off corner.

"For Pete's sake," father thought, "more animals and those big horses at that." He walked to the back of the barn to open the door of the horses' pen.

Fortunately the horses were not tied up and came outside on their own. Just when father wanted to close the door to prevent the horses from going back inside, a little foal stuck her head around the corner of the door and whinnied softly for her mother. The mother, who already missed her little one, hummed softly and the little animal jumped outside. Quickly father closed the door and walked to the basement. He was tired out.

"Go to sleep for a while," mother said, "I'll stay awake."

But sleeping was out of the question.

A little later they heard a tremendous explosion. It made the ground rumble. When Jan peered through the little basement window he saw some distance away the sky colored red with the fire that followed the explosion. When he saw from which direction the blaze of the fire came he went to father and said, "The ammunition barn at Berenpas' was blown up. How will the farmer, his wife and Gerrit-Jan be getting along?"

"I don't know son. We'll have to wait for the new day and then we'll see. Now we can't do anything," father answered resignedly.

The Liberation

By about five o'clock that morning the shooting slowed down and a little later stopped all together. When father looked through the basement window he saw shadows sneaking through the garden. They were Canadian soldiers with their typical flat helmets and black faces.

"The reconnaissance troops are walking around the house," father said. "Keep as far away from the basement door as possible. You never know how they will react when they hear or see something."

For half an hour it was deadly silent. Suddenly Ina sat up straight.

"Father, I hear cars and tanks on the road."

"Thank goodness," father said, "then they are marching on and the front is passing us. That means we're liberated."

Involuntarily he had to think about the war of 1914-1918. Then he had been a soldier himself for four long years. Walking patrol every night on the Belgian border, with the knowledge that there had to be an invisible enemy. He felt a deep respect for the liberators.

When full daylight had come father left the basement to make an inspection. On the clay road in front of the farm a long column of military vehicles rumbled without interruption. They all had a large star on the side and one on the roof of the vehicles.

"Come out of the basement now mother," father called, "and bring the children along."

Mother took Jaap in her arms and went outside. The children ran to the front of the house to wave at the soldiers. The soldiers waved back and threw cookies and chocolate to the children and cigarettes to father.

Father and Jan went behind the farmhouse to see if much damage had been caused and where all the cattle had gone. The cows walked quietly in the field. Two had been hit by shrapnel and lay dead. The foal frolicked around her mother. In the meantime it was twelve noon and the number of passing cars and tanks slowed down.

From the other direction however arrived military cars with a red cross.

"Where are they going?" Jan asked. "They transport the dead and wounded soldiers to the field hospitals. Because even though we don't see any dead soldiers," father said, "don't think there aren't any. In a while you'll be shocked about the number of dead Canadians. Yes son, and that to liberate us. Come we'll go eat and then later we'll look at our belongings at farmer Berenpas'."

Around three o'clock that afternoon—the family was just ready to go back to their previous shelter at farmer Berenpas'—the farmer with his wife and daughter drove into the farmyard.

"Good day," was all they said. They parked their bikes against the front of the house and went inside.

"Kindness means a lot," father said, "let's go." And so the whole family walked for the second time through the fields, but now back home.

When they walked into the farmyard and stood eye to eye with the ruins, tears came to their eyes. Of the barn that had served as storage of ammunition nothing was to be found. A deep crater in the ground showed the place where the barn had been. The little shed where the Deurwaarders had lived was badly damaged and unlivable. While the old chicken shed where they had slept had collapsed onto the beds.

"Terrible," mother sighed, "now what?"

Farmer Berenpas came towards them with outstretched hands.

"How are you?" he asked, "have you come through all right?"

"Yes," father said, "thankfully nobody has a scratch. But how did you get along?"

"Fine," the farmer said, "there was terrible fighting in the Elze woods. An hour before the Canadians arrived we went into the bomb shelter where you also were. We were hardly inside when the Germans blew up the barn with the ammunition. So you see again, desperate needs lead to desperate deeds."

While father and mother were talking Jan quietly cleared out to the Elze woods. The woods teemed with Canadians. Large field kitchens stood under the trees and many tents around them. It smelled delicious, like roast chicken and beef. Jan walked farther into the woods and saw in several places dead German soldiers. A German soldier sat at the edge of the woods with binoculars in his hands. His helmet had fallen over his face and hung under his chin, full of blood. In his head was a little hole. The man still looked alive. A Canadian sniper had killed him. A little farther was the body of a German soldier. His head was detached. Somebody told Jan that the soldier had exploded a hand grenade next to his head. A few meters away from him lay his helmet, only the skull was still inside.

"Terrible," Jan thought, "to finish off your life in such a way."

There were no dead Canadian soldiers, they had already been moved.

While walking around, Jan's hands were filled with food. Quickly he took it to mother, so everyone would get something. The white bread especially was delicious.

Homeless Again

"And now you stay here, Jan," father said, "there is work to be done. We have to get as much furniture as possible from under the ruins, because we may still need that later." From under the collapsed roof the bedding was retrieved and shaken out as well as possible. They could not do much more about it. Meanwhile Berenpas came to stand with them.

"You can't stay here tonight," he said. "Take your bedding and most valuable possessions and go to the porch. The family that lived there have left and I don't know when they'll come back. Tomorrow is another day."

On the floor of the porch beds were made up and everyone had a small space. The children soon fell asleep. But father and mother tossed for a while. "What would the future bring?"

The next morning one of Berenpas' sons came to father and said: "I know about a house for you."

"Oh, really," father said in surprise, "where is it?"

"If you turn left at the other side of the train track you arrive at the signal man's house after fifteen minutes. The last inhabitant was a N.S.B. member. Nobody knows where the family is, but they are not allowed back in."

"Thanks," father said, "we'll go and have a look."

Father with Jan and Wim went to have a look. After an hour they were back.

"Indeed," father said to mother. "A very comfortable home and even furnished. Everything was left unlocked as if the people left in a big hurry."

"Well," mother said, "we need something, let's take the risk." Quickly some buckets and rags and a sponge and chamois-leather were found. Some sandwiches were put in a bag and then the family left in procession to the new house. As best they could they cleaned the whole thing.

"As long as we can sleep again," mother thought, "the rest will follow."

When at around seven o'clock that evening the house was pretty well ready and they were eating a sandwich, the front door was opened.

"Good evening," a strange man said, who stepped inside together with his wife and two children.

"Who are you and what are you doing in our house?"

Father and mother changed color. The children kept stock-still.

"We thought we could live here for a while," father said. "They ruined our house. We were sent here and we were told that the man who had lived here was a N.S.B. member and would be in jail now.

"Well, that's too bad for you," the man answered. "I have been part of the N.S.B. but I was no member of the party. So nobody can touch me. But thanks for cleaning the house. Now you can leave again."

Father and mother could do nothing else than pack their things and very dejectedly go back to the farm of Berenpas.

There they were allowed to sleep in the barn that night, because the people who used the porch had returned as well.

That evening, it was already very late, Aaldering the neighbor of Berenpas came by.

He said: "I know what you're up against. Come by tomorrow, I have a number of large chicken barns of which some are empty. You can use one of those till you can go back to your ship."

"That would be great," father said, "we will gladly come and have a look."

The next morning father and mother went to the neighbor to see what he had to offer. Ina had to watch the children and Jan had to help Gerrit-Jan, otherwise there would be trouble, according to mother. But Jan quickly sneaked away again to the Canadians in the woods.

Farmer Aalderink received father and mother and introduced them to his wife. Next the four of them went to the orchard where the chicken barns were, to look at the future shelter. It turned out to be a large chicken shed, where, beside a living area, two little bedrooms could also be made. With a little making do they could easily live there. They told Aalderink that they would gladly use the chicken shed and that they wanted to clean it as soon as possible. Mother and Ina worked hard and cleaned it in one day. Father and Jan meanwhile did some carpentry work and hung up old curtains in front of the windows and for dividers between the sleeping areas. The next morning the possessions that were left were brought over by horse and wagon from farmer Berenpas' to the chicken shed and decorating could start.

After everything was in reasonable order and a few children went to school in Eefde, mother got lonesome for the two children in Wemeldinge: Johan and Rie. For almost a year nothing had been heard from them. How were they doing? After discussing it with father, mother determined to find out and went on a trip together with Wim. Walking and hitchhiking to Arnhem and from there on by train to Den Bosch. They stayed overnight at the station in Den Bosch and the next morning on to Wemeldinge. Everyone was delighted to see each other. For tante De Vos also it was reassuring to see one another in good health.

On the way home mother soon found out that hitchhiking with two people is easier than with four. The beginning of the return trip started badly. In the afternoon not one train left Goes in the direction of Bergen op Zoom. To return to Wemelding until the next morning would take too much time. So it was decided they would sleep at the station in Goes in an empty train. Because of the hard seats they were lying on, without blankets or heat, they woke early. But finally the train left. However, that day they got no further than Arnhem, where they were received by people of the Red Cross. They had some empty houses available where stranded travelers could stay overnight. It was already well past noon on the following day when they arrived hitchhiking and walking in Eefde. Only then was the family reunited again.

Meanwhile Wim had found his cup of tea. The exploded ammunition train and the heavy fighting between the Canadians and the Germans meant that unexploded ammunition was lying around everywhere. Whole shoulder-belts with bullets were taken home and hidden by him, because if father found out he would be sorry. Using the vice he took the bullets out of the cases. He shook the powder out of the cases and saved it in a little jar. The percussion-caps he exploded with a hammer and nail.

The light ammunition he liked the best. He looked for a piece of metal pipe that fit the case exactly. The pipe was attached to a piece of wood in such a way that it pointed up at an angle. Then the percussion-cap was exploded with a hammer and nail. After a short, dry bang and much hissing the light bullet made a nice big arch. The saved powder was sprinkled over the ground in different shapes and lit. Especially in the dark, when unsuspecting people came by, this had a nice effect. Fortunately it all ended well. But how many did not have to pay for this recklessness with death or bodily harm?

Father Looks For Work

One night when they were all together for the first time in their new home father said, "Tomorrow I'm going to look if there is work to be had. First I'll go to Eefde and if that doesn't work out to Zutphen. Because as long as we don't know where the Orion is I'll have to earn our bread and butter somewhere else."

But that was disappointing. In Eefde he went to several businesses but nowhere were people ready to start producing again. The wounds of the war were too fresh. The next day he went out again, by bike to Zutphen. The shortest way to Zutphen was not usable anymore, because the bridge over the canal had been blown up by the Germans. So it was necessary to make a detour via the locks in Eefde and over Warnsveld. That meant almost four extra kilometers.

But of course that counted not only for father. All the people who worked in Zutphen had that problem and also the school children who went to Zutphen to secondary school. And suddenly father discovered there the work he was looking for. He could operate a little ferry next to the collapsed bridge over the canal. However he could not do that by himself and therefore contacted an other skipper living on shore, whose ship had sunk. When father suggested they construct a passenger ferry that skipper was immediately enthusiastic.

First, materials were bought and transported to the canal. Eight large oil drums were attached to each other and enclosed with a wooden frame. On top of that a sturdy floor was laid and a trustworthy handrail attached on both sides. Over the whole surface of the ferry they tied a tarp so people would stay dry during the crossing. Lastly, a steel cable had to be stretched over the canal along which the ferry could be pulled back and forth. A fortunate circumstance was that father's colleague could get quite a bit of material from his ship which was not totally submerged.

When the construction was finished the ferry was put into the water with the help of some bystanders. The trial run went well. It had good stability and could be pulled ahead quickly with the steel cable.

Now wait and see. Would there be much interest? Would the people be willing to pay a small fee? Sure enough. The first day only those came who knew a ferry was being built, but the mouth to mouth advertising worked great. In no time school children lined up morning and afternoon. During rush hour they had their hands full. And so father could earn his own bread and butter and he did not have to depend on others.

On the ferry was the following inscription:

*If I had Solomon's brain
and Samson's brawn,
still I could not sail
to please everyone.*

He could operate a little ferry next to the collapsed bridge over the canal.

The Foreman

Right after the family moved into the chicken shed Jan started working for farmer Aalderink. Workers were not yet available. Many young men who were at the right age had been deported and were not home yet and many would never come home again. Besides that, the government had already made arrangements to send many young Dutch men to the former Dutch East Indies.

Jan did his best and pleased farmer Aalderink. They worked from six o'clock in the morning till twelve o'clock and from two o'clock in the afternoon until eight o'clock at night. Those were long days, but the work was satisfying. Three horses in front of the grain-harvester was something spectacular to Jan. But taking a big bull from the field, while it was snorting dangerously, was too much for him.

The Aalderink family consisted of the father and mother and three children. The father was a fervent horse lover. A large prize-cupboard hung full with beautiful prizes. Horse-showing was his first love. Father Aalderink hoped his oldest son would follow in his footsteps and also ride horses. When he turned twelve he was given a full-blooded horse. It was brought all the way from Maastricht to Eefde. The boy thought it a nice present, but nothing more. That was not enough for such a horse. It was an animal with temperament and she was happy to show it.

"Well, if you don't want to," the farmer said to his son, "Jan would love to." And so Jan, who already looked after the horse, had the chance to ride it.

Clean-up of the War Damage

Shortly after the liberation the government machinery came into action again. The State Water Control (Rijkswaterstaat) also got busy. There was a lot of work to be done. All the wrecks still in the Twente canal had to be made floatable and transported to different shipyards. Many of these ship were seriously damaged under the water-line. Many had innumerable bullet holes. Others were bombed and as a result had broken up. Besides that the locks in Eefde had to be repaired, as well as the bridge lying in the canal. Indeed no ships could pass. An enormous job at first glance. A great many derricks would be needed to finish all this work. And there were no derricks. What was left had to be used first in the seaports, the life blood of the Dutch economy.

Then they got the unique idea of emptying the whole Twente canal between Eefde and the lock in Goor. The sunken ships would automatically empty through the bullet holes. There would not even be any derricks needed. The bullet holes could be temporarily plugged while the ship was on the bottom. And when later the water came back into the canal they would float again on their own. At the same time the State Water Control (Rijkswaterstaat) could inspect the canal bottom and if necessary remove the war materials left behind.

This would also work for the locks in Eefde. Because a dry lock-floor would be quicker and easier to clean and repair. And so it happened. One day the canal was pretty well dry. Only in the deepest spots was a little water left behind, to the relief of many fish. The lock also dried up. To everyone's' amazement, after the last liters of water drained away, a large part of a V2 became visible. How did it get there? Nobody had ever seen it fall. Maybe it was dragged along by a ship.

After several months the work on the lock and the canal was so far advanced that the water could be replenished. The lock-doors were replaced and closed. The shipwrecks were temporarily closed up. Then the pumping-engines were turned on. It took an enormous amount of power, because the water had to be pumped up to a height of about ten meters. Pumping continued day and night for one week and then the water in the canal reached the same level as before.

Slowly shipping started up again. Many damaged ships were back in service again and took part in transportation. Sand, gravel, and cement were especially needed to repair the damage.

Sailing on the little ferry father saw all the ships come by. Therefore his thoughts were often somewhere else. "Where could the Orion have gone? How could she have disappeared without a trace? Would it have been better if he had stayed on board?"

The Orion Is Found

Half a year after liberation there was a knock on the door of the chicken shed one night. Father opened the door. A strange man stood in front of the door.

"Are you Deurwaarder of the Orion?" he asked father.

"Yes, indeed," father said, "I am."

He shook father's hand and said, "My name is Vinder of the motorship Nooit Gedacht."

"Come in," father said, "the coffee is ready."

After everyone had found a chair, the man said, "you used to sail on the Orion in the past?"

"Sure thing," father said, "but that is quite a while ago and we still have not heard anything since the Germans commandeered it. Do you know anything about it?"

"Maybe," the man said. "Last week I was in Groningen with my ship. When I went for a bike ride along the canal I saw a ship that looked exactly like the Orion."

"Didn't it have a name?" father asked.

"No," the man said, "the ship is burned out and red with rust. Even the name on the bow has peeled in such a way that it isn't readable anymore. I understand it is not pleasant news for you that she is burned out, but now you know what is going on. Otherwise you might keep on searching and asking with much uncertainty."

"Yes, you are right," father said. "I'll go and have a look on Monday. Many thanks anyway for taking the trouble to come and let us know. If you are still here on Sunday with your ship, bring your wife and children for a cup of coffee."

"I'll think about it," the man said. He shook hands with father and mother and left.

That Saturday and Sunday father was restless. Everyone was in his way and hardly got an answer when a question was asked. His thoughts were with the Orion. What would he find? If you believed that man it was one chunk of rust and what could you do with that?

That Monday morning he left Eefde early. He went by bicycle to Zutphen. The little ferry had been taken out of service by then. An emergency bridge had been constructed for passengers and cyclists. In Zutphen he took the train to Groningen. Shortly after noon he arrived there. At the station he rented a bike and drove along the canal in the direction of Stroobos. "If only I am biking on the right side of the canal," he said to himself. "There aren't many bridges and then I may have to make a long detour yet too."

After biking for half an hour he saw something in the distance in the canal that looked like a ship. As he got closer it became more and more obvious that it was indeed a ship. After another ten minutes biking he came to the place and saw a ship, or rather, something that used to be a ship. There was nothing left but a rusted hulk. The sides of the ship were curved by the heat and the decks looked like wrinkled cardboard. The thick glass of the port-holes had melted. But father had seen meanwhile that it was his ship, his Orion. Defeated he stood looking for a while. What could he do with that? Would it be possible to rebuild?

Father looked around and saw at a distance behind the canal dike a farm. He got back on his bike and drove over. He knocked on the backdoor. A man with a Gronings accent opened the door and asked, "What do you want?"

Father said, "My name is Deurwaarder, I am the owner of the burned out ship that's lying in the canal here."

"Oh yes, right," the farmer said, "Come on in."

While the farmer's wife poured coffee the farmer related that a few days before liberation the ship had been put there by the Germans.

"On board there were two German soldiers and a civilian. The civilian, he was the skipper, came here to get milk. He said that he had been apprehended in Meppel by the Germans because he had left his ship behind in Rotterdam. He was ordered to take your ship to Germany via Groningen. He said that there were four hundred barrels of gin in the ship. The soldiers had been very scared and quickly wanted to sail to Germany.

"'That's impossible,' the skipper had said, 'the ship lies much too deep to be able to sail through the lock. First a part of the load has to be unloaded.' The soldiers who also listened to the radio, knew that the Allied armies had pushed on to Zwolle. Only a few more days and they would be in Groningen and then they would be caught. 'Yes, and then you won't be so well off,' the skipper had frightened them. The next morning one of the soldiers stopped a car at the bottom of the canal dike. 'Get in,' he said to the skipper. To the chauffeur he said to wait, because someone else was coming. He walked up the dike and called something to his colleague.

"A little later we heard an heavy explosion followed by a fierce fire. The Hun had thrown a hand grenade into the hold of the ship, jumped into the waiting car, and driven away toward Groningen.

"I went to look at the edge of the water," the farmer related, "but the fire was so intense that because of the heat you had to stay at a distance of one hundred meters. The road along the canal was out of service for forty eight hours because of the heat."

The Fuss

"Thanks for your information," father said, "I'll contact my insurance company and will have to ask the authorities for permission to sail away from here."

"I'm sorry," the farmer said, "that's the way it is, good luck."

To get his ship back father had to report to the Allied army of occupation in Groningen. Together with someone who spoke English father went to the military head-quarters.

But that was disappointment number two. "Your ship was loaded with German goods," the Canadian commander said, "and so your ship is spoils of war. Come back tomorrow at 10:00 o'clock. Meanwhile I'll have had contact with the officer who looks after these matters. I can probably tell you then how much it will cost you to get your ship back."

Early next morning father and the translator stood on the steps of the military commander. He put a document in front of him, which showed that father could take his ship after payment of 350 guilders.

There was no other choice but to pay. Father went to the bank, took out the money and paid the commander. After they both signed, father got the original document. The commander shook father's hand and wished him, "Good luck."

But now the Orion had to be moved from there.

"Where do I go with it?" father thought.

He remembered that there was a good size dockyard in Hoogkerk of the Brakmeyer brothers. By bike he drove there. After telling them what had happened to the Orion they thought it pretty obvious that the ship would be brought to the dockyard. Father could then wait quietly until the insurance company decided about the amount of compensation.

"We also have a tugboat with the dockyard," they said, "and if you don't mind we will get the ship and put it here."

"That is wonderful," father said, "I'll go back to my wife and children and keep you informed about what will happen next."

And so father went back home. A few days later he left by train for Rotterdam to talk to the Shipsmortgage Bank and the insurance company. The result was not promising. The insurance was based on the value of the new ship. However, that was much less than the repair costs would add up to. All prices rose dramatically right after the war, and so also dockyard repairs. Before father could talk with the Shipsmortgage Bank about a mortgage he had to know first what the repairs would cost. He contacted the dockyard in Groningen and asked for a quick estimate of the cost of repairs. After a few days father was called and was told that the repairs would add up to about 48,000 guilders. With that information father went back to the bank and asked how big a mortgage they could give him. The bank turned out to be very obliging. Because father had always faithfully made his mortgage payments on time, he was promised a loan that would be more than enough for the repairs of the Orion. With these positive messages father went back home to discuss it with mother. Many of the pros and cons were discussed as well as the possibility of emigrating to Canada. But father wondered what they would need a skipper for in Canada. Finally it was decided to have the Orion repaired and put back into the water.

A Hard Winter

Again father went to the North to discuss matters with the managers of the Brakmeyer dockyard. He told them that the mortgage was available and that the Shipsmortgage Bank would give guarantees for the repairs. So that should not be a problem for them.

"So, that is solved," father said. "Another question is whether you can repair such a big ship in a medium-sized dockyard? And if so, do you want to?"

"While you were away," they said to father, "we looked the situation over and discussed this with our personnel. The slips are exactly long enough to turn the Orion. We'll pull it as high as possible and put it on heavy skids. After that we can lower the slips again to use for other work. Our personnel has had nothing to do for so long during the last year of the war that they are happy there is work again. They would gladly work on the repairs."

"When can you start and how long will these repairs take?" father asked. "We can start right away," the yard foreman said. "We'll put a permanent crew on your ship and the others can pitch in when they have nothing else to do. If we can work continuously we estimate it will take half a year. What we don't have any control over is the delivery of materials. Everything has to get going again and all dockyards are screaming for steel."

"Then I have one more question," father said, "where can I live with my family in the meantime?"

"We can take care of that too," the manager said, "unless you want to live in the village."

"Well, that isn't exactly necessary," father said. "As long as the children can walk to school, it doesn't matter very much where we live."

"Come along," the manager said. And together they strolled to the back of the grounds.

"Look," he said, "here is a good size empty office-shed. If it is big enough for your family you can use it."

After father walked through the shed he said, "I think it will be big enough, we'll have to make do, but we can do that. We would gladly use it."

"That's fine," the manager said, "next week you can move in."

"Great," father said.

Some more information was exchanged about the school and the church. The manager promised father he would contact the headmaster of the Christian school.

"Fine," father said, "then I'll go home now to get everything ready to come here." He shook hands with the manager, thanked him for his cooperation and left.

When he got home father had a lot to tell. Everyone was curious and wanted to know everything. Especially the children who would be going to school again in Hoogkerk. But father said that he did not know about it either. He had not seen a school and had not spoken to a teacher. Wait and see.

But first a lot had to be done. Farmer Aalderink had to be informed about the coming move of the family. A moving date had to be set and a moving van had to be found.

"And," father said to Jan, "what do you want to do? Farmer Aalderink would like you to keep working for him, but do you feel like it?"

"No," Jan said, "I don't want to stay here. I rather go along to Hoogkerk."

"That's fine," father said, "there is surely some work to be found for you."

In the fall of 1946 all the furniture of the Deurwaarders was loaded onto a moving van and they left for the north. Another episode in their life was closed.

When, after driving for hours, they arrived in Hoogkerk and approached the dockyard, they could see from some distance the Orion on the shore. The ship stuck out above all the sheds. The furniture was put on top of some rugs in the future home and the driver left for Zutphen. Because, meanwhile, evening had arrived, it seemed best to mother to make some beds on the floor, then they could at least sleep that night and the next morning cleaning could be started. Three beds were made next to each other on the floor and that night everyone slept well, tired as they were from the long trip in that bouncing moving van.

The next morning after breakfast, mother and Ina went hard at work to clean the office-shed. Jan had to carry warm water and watch the little ones. But that did not last long.

"Those little ones can look after themselves," Jan thought, "I'm going to have a look on the Orion."

When father saw Jan poking around he said, "What are you doing here? Aren't you supposed to help mother?"

"Oh, yes," Jan said, "but there isn't much to do and the little ones can look after themselves."

But that went down the wrong way with father. "Go on. For now you will help your mother. You can come back here lots of times after today," he railed against Jan.

By evening the office-shed was magically changed into a comfortable little home. Not very big for such a large family, but after all you can get many willing sheep in a pen. The next morning father took the children, except Ina, Jan and Wim, to school for the first time. Afterwards there was no more time for that and they had to find their own way. It was a long walk over the cold dike in the Groningen countryside.

The repairs on the Orion went quickly. All the rivets in the plates at the side of the ship were burned loose and removed. Then the plates were taken to a shed and turned through an enormous plate-roller. That made them a lot smoother; most of the bubbles disappeared. Everything went smoothly till winter started. Then the work pretty well stopped. The metal could not be worked. Many people were sent home. Within a week there was a layer of ice sixty centimeters thick on the canal. The children enjoyed the fun on the ice, even if they almost froze their ears and toes. But father was not happy. A hard, long winter meant a serious delay in the finishing of the Orion and thus also in having an income. And a family of eleven people could use quite a large income. He kept busy with the work on the ship, in spite of the harsh cold. Ina could not be missed and had to help mother.

But there was nothing for Jan to do. "This can't go on any longer," father said, "eating but not working, we'll have to do something about that."

Father went to the dockyard manager and told him what was going on.

"You want Jan to start working?" he asked father.

"Indeed," father said, "this hanging around is no good."

"Wait a minute," he said to father. He took the phone and dialed a number. After a moment the receiver was put down.

He took father along to the window, pointed outside and said, "you see that chimney smoking over there?"

"Certainly," father said.

"That is a laundry," he said, "a friend of mine is the manager there. Go over there. Tomorrow morning at seven o'clock Jan can start work if he wants to."

Together they went. The manager of the laundry did not have much time.

"He can start tomorrow," he said to father, "we work from seven o'clock in the morning till five o'clock at night. He will earn nine guilders a week."

"You want to do that?" father asked Jan.

"Oh, I may as well try," Jan said, "better than nothing. At least it is inside." And so a new life started for Jan—hired hand in a laundry.

The first morning he was put behind a large press. This was used to iron the sheets. There was no end to them. It was very hot in the laundry and the air was so stuffy with all the steam, that it was sometimes impossible to take. The days were long. Leave home in the dark and return in the dark. Jan longed for spring. After three months that seemed like years, the frost subsided and the days got a little longer.

"Wait a bit," father said to Jan, "as soon as we can work outside you can leave there and you can start working on board ship."

After several weeks the time came.

"Tell your boss that next week will be your last. Then he can start looking for someone else," father said one day.

That did not fall on deaf ears. And so Jan started working on board the Orion.

By the end of April the ship was so far ready that it could be taken to the engine factory of Brons in Appingedam. The engine had been dismantled earlier and taken to the factory by truck and was like new, waiting to be installed again. Once it arrived there everybody thought it would be ready in a few weeks. But they could forget that. It turned out that all the copper tubing had either melted because of the heat or suffered so much that it had to be replaced. So that job took another six weeks. The trial trip went well.

First everything was made ready for sailing and then father went to inquire if there was anything to load. But that was not so simple. Everyone expected that there would be lots of work after the war, but that was a miscalculation. In the north there was nothing to load.

"So, that's not such a good start," father said. "Then we'll first sail to Zwolle."

After two days they arrived, but there was nothing doing the ship-charterer said at the exchange. "There is nothing coming up either; I wouldn't wait if I were you."

Then they sailed on to Arnhem, but it was the same thing there. Finally they ended up in Maasbracht. There they had to wait another three weeks before they could load.

Jan Leaves Ship

Meanwhile three children had left again for school in Wemeldinge. Ina had left ship too and had taken a position in Zutphen. "And," father said to Jan, "shortly your younger brother comes back from school and I have no room for two sailors. We will look out for another ship for you."

After a few weeks father came back from the shipping-exchange.

"Listen Jan," he said, "I have been talking to a good acquaintance and he is looking for a hired hand. Will that be something for you?"

"I guess it will have to be," Jan said.

When they were in Dordrecht a few days later they saw the ship Jan would be sailing on. He packed his suitcases and left. For the hundredth time a new way of life started. But at the same time a momentous period of his life became history.

....

Made in the USA
Lexington, KY
19 November 2019